# FICTION -V- REALITY

# FICTION -V- REALITY

JEZABEL NIGHTINGALE

Join the reader newsletter for more authors that have taken a stand against the use of AI-generated content: https://www.authenticityinitiative.com/for-readers

ISBN 978-0-6458061-7-5 (Paperback)
ISBN 978-0-6458061-8-2 (e-Book)

Edited by Sarah Baker, The Word Emporium
Proofread by Cheyenne Sampson, Frogg Spa Editing
Cover art by Kristin Barrett, K. B. Barrett Designs

jezabelnightingale.com

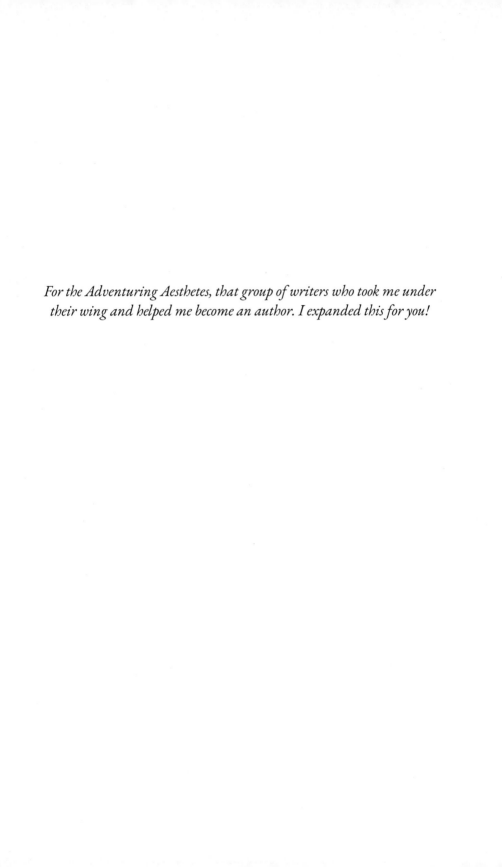

*For the Adventuring Aesthetes, that group of writers who took me under their wing and helped me become an author. I expanded this for you!*

"Fiction is the lie through which we tell the truth."

Albert Camus

# Before you start...

This book is set in the Southern Hemisphere where seasons are back to front compared to our European and American friends. School and university years start in January/February and end in November/December with the summer holidays happening over Christmas. There may be 'Australianisms' that make little sense to you, please feel free to reach out in my Facebook group, or via email, if you need clarification!

# Val

ALMOST EVERYONE IN THE OFFICE WOULD HAVE PREFERRED A Christmas party, but instead, the partners decided that a weekend team building exercise in early January would be a much better idea.

"It's left up here," I tell Janet, my friend from university who I'm fortunate to work with. She's driving us in her new Mercedes, a Christmas gift from her girlfriend, Penny. It may be ostentatious, but it's bloody comfortable.

"What have you forgotten?" Janet chuckles as the gates to the holiday camp come into view.

It's a long-standing joke that I forget things. It's not that I forget, but my mind is full of too many important things to remember the mundane. I've packed my toothbrush and clothes, but I know she's right. I've forgotten something.

"Um..." I trail off as we pass under a banner that tells us we are entering the Spirited Heights Village. I had hoped that it was Halloween themed, but indeed it is a Christian-run facility. "Was I meant to bring *Twister*?"

"Yep, but I don't think we'll miss *that* game." Janet laughs. "I've got the Australian version of *Monopoly*, because Sandra says you can't play anything but the original, and I plan to show her."

Sandra is one of the legal secretaries. She's worked for the firm for over twenty years, starting when her youngest started school. She'll tell people that yes, she's that old.

Janet parks her car as far away from the entrance to the main hall as possible, claiming she can't park under a gum tree in case it sheds a limb or drops sap on her precious black paint.

Spirited Heights is in the Gold Coast Hinterland, a bit of a drive from our Brisbane office, but it's a little cooler up here than down by the coast. As I step out of the car, though, it's clear the flies and mosquitos know we're easy targets.

The gravel crunches under my feet as we walk towards the entrance of a large building that looks like it has seen countless groups like ours come through its doors in the spirit of team building and goal setting. The wire door creaks as I open it, ushering Janet through in front of me. She has her hands full with a suitcase, cosmetic bag, and laptop bag, with the board game wedged under her arm. I've only got the one bag. I'm not one for excessive makeup and skin care, but I rub some moisturiser into my face each night. It's not like I'm getting any younger after all.

"Ah, Valerie and Janet," Katherine, one of the senior partners, greets us as we enter the large foyer. She's sitting at a makeshift desk that has everything arranged neatly and in some sense of order. "I'm glad you didn't get lost, although I assume you drove, Janet?"

"Of course she did, Katherine." I laugh. "But, alas, I did forget to bring *Twister*."

"I think we'll make do." Katherine smiles as she scans her sheet, a beautifully manicured finger sliding down the page to find our names. "Now, you're both on the second floor. I figure you young ones can climb the stairs better than us oldies."

Katherine is in her midsixties and has no plans to retire anytime soon. My parents are of a similar age and have already bought a unit to retire to. I can't see Dad retiring in the near future, but I know Mum's itching to, having already decreased her work schedule by a day a week.

"Right, you two." Katherine claps her hands. "209 and 211. It doesn't really matter who takes what room, but I have put you at the end with the bathrooms. There's a key hanging on the back of the doors, so feel free to lock up when you leave, but don't feel you need to if you think you'll lose the key." Katherine looks directly at me with a grin on her face. She claims I'm the reason they went to electronic locks at the office, but I never managed to not find a key I'd misplaced, even if it took a week or so.

"I assume you've read the rules I sent you?" Janet and I look at each other and shrug. I haven't read anything about the weekend, except when it was on and that I'd been given Friday off. Most of us have, except for a few who had cases they're working on and chose to take Monday instead. "No alcohol on-site and no fraternisation in the bedrooms."

"Just the bedrooms?" I ask with a grin, knowing there's no way I'd fraternise with anyone from work. It's a rule I set myself when I became a lawyer. I love sex as much as the next person, but usually I have short, meaningless flings or pick someone up at a bar. I'm not about to shit where I eat, so to speak.

Katherine rolls her eyes, her lips curling up as she taps the milk crate on the ground that looks like an alcoholic's wet dream. "Right, you two, first things first, alcohol. Hand it over."

"Who brought the 25-year-old scotch?" I ask as I pull out some bottles inquisitively.

"Max." Katherine shakes her head at her husband's antics. "There's another one in there from Rhys, too."

Rhys is one of the new partners. He came on board towards the end of last year and deals with maritime law. He's not in the office a lot, and I've never really taken the time to get to know him.

I deal with family law. It makes me see why, at almost thirty, I'm nowhere near marrying or settling down, much to the chagrin of my family. They're all in wonderful, deliriously happy marriages, and I know that I'll end up the statistic that ends in divorce. At least I'll know how to make sure I get everything I'm entitled to if it ever comes to that.

Janet places a bottle of vodka in the crate, writing her name on a swing tag that she hangs from the neck. I'd not even thought to pack alcohol, so I can't really say I forgot it.

"Next thing..." Katherine weaves her fingers together on the table. "Phones." She unclasps her hands and opens a box I hadn't seen sitting on her desk. "You didn't read the paperwork, did you?" We're both chided, and based on the looks of shock on our faces, Janet hasn't been paying attention to the rules for this weekend either.

I hesitantly place my phone in the box. It's covered in a fluorescent yellow case. It was a secret Santa gift from someone in my family who thought it would mean I never lost my phone again. I think it's ugly enough that no one would dare touch it, but at least I know there's no need to label it, as it really is one of a kind.

A sigh escapes my mouth as I look at it sitting amongst the other black, navy, and brown cases. To be honest, it will be nice being uncontactable by my family this weekend. I love them to bits, but they can be a little intense. They're all up in Cassowary Point, the town I grew up in, and can't see why I'm still in Brisbane after almost thirteen years.

As much as I adore my job and the people I work with, I'd go home tomorrow to be closer to them all if they'd only shut up about my love life. It's bad enough that I didn't go into medicine like all of them and keep being ribbed about it, but they seem to think I'll only be happy being married to a doctor like they all are.

"Can I just ring Penny?" Janet grips her phone for dear life, and Katherine shoos her outside to make the call.

Janet moved in with me ten years ago and lived in the apartment my parents own in Brisbane whilst we finished uni. Penny, the daughter of someone my parents know, was moving down here and moved in with us, and she and Janet have been inseparable ever since. When I moved into my cottage almost five years ago, Janet and Penny bought a gorgeous condo that overlooks the water.

Penny's made it big in the art world, both as a painter and a sculptor. Her father is incredibly wealthy, and I suspect that's how she got her start. Even so, her work is amazing, and it's not surprising it's so highly sought after.

With another set of the rules for the weekend in my hands, I make my way up the stairs to our floor, thinking about how, at times, I'm jealous of Janet and Penny and their relationship. It seems like almost everyone in my life is partnered up and living their best life. I'd like to think I'm living my best life too, it just looks different from other people's. It's not like I need a significant other or children to make me happy. I have a kick-ass career. I have friends, and I have amazing nieces.

As I walk along the corridor, I smile, realising how different this is from what I imagined when it was first suggested. I'd envisaged a tropical resort with cocktails by the pool. This is anything but.

I choose the room nearest the bathroom. It's tiny, with a single bed that has a cross perched over it. A picture of Jesus is on the opposite wall, with posters that look like they've been on the walls for years, quoting Bible passages with photos of mountains, sunsets, and kittens.

The pillow is lumpy, and the bedsprings creak when I sit on the edge.

This could be an interesting weekend.

"Welcome, welcome." Katherine stands at the front of the hall we've gathered in as per our timetable. Her hands are clasped together like she's itching to have fun. It's hard not to be infected with her optimism and *joie de vivre*. Max looks at her like she hung the moon and all the stars, the same way my parents gaze at each other.

They've never had children, even though I think both of them would be amazing parents, and I figure if they can make the most of their life without reproducing, then I should be able to, too. I'm not sure my body agrees, though. It's been harder since my bestie, Emily, who is married to my brother, Boyd, had a baby almost six months ago. They'd been trying for years. Baby Isobel is just gorgeous and another reason I'd love to move back to Cassowary Point. Sure, I FaceTime them, but it's not the same as getting baby snuggles.

I'll be thirty next month, and whilst I know it's not that old in the scheme of reproductiveness, I'd need someone to father a child. Maybe I need to bite the bullet and go to a sperm bank and withdraw a deposit. Doing it alone in Brisbane is scary, though. Janet and Penny have been talking children, and whilst it would be nice to have them together, I couldn't expect a lot of support from them if they were busy with their own baby. I'd be relying on childcare and hoping my parents would visit and help out. My sex life would disappear, that's for sure. There's no way I'd bring a guy home, let alone with a baby in the house, and it's unfair to hire a sitter so I can get my needs satisfied.

My attention is brought back to the front of the room where Katherine has been talking about the different activities they planned for the weekend. I feel like I'm on school camp with talk of high ropes and low ropes, but I think I heard something about a fire pit and damper. I love baking, so I'll probably sign up for that.

"Lastly, dinner is almost ready." Katherine smiles as if all her family is gathered together for once. We are her family, I suppose, and I need to make sure we make this a wonderful weekend for everyone, especially her and Max. "It's been catered by Raw Delites, a local vegan catering firm, and the menu sounds divine."

"That's it," Janet whispers in my ear. "Fried food and beer Sunday night when this is over. This is the worst idea in the history of ideas. If I'd known that was what your firm was like, I never would have interviewed or accepted a job here."

I know she's joking. She loves her job in contract law, and working with her for the last year or so has been great.

As we move next door to the dining room, I'm surprised by the spread in front of us. It actually looks and smells amazing. Janet settles on the Vietnamese-style salad with marinated mushrooms, and I go for the warm Moroccan tofu and vegetables served with rice.

We're not the first in the dining room, but those who were here before us have snagged tables together. I was expecting long tables with chairs on either side, but it's café style. I see Sandra has pushed two tables together and gathered a few of the secretaries together, along with two older lawyers on the team.

Janet and I escape to the far end of the room and sit at a table for four, almost hoping no one joins us. Our hope is short-lived, as Janet waves people over, a smile on her face. I should have sat on the opposite side so I can see, but my back is to whoever she gestures to.

"Can we join you?" Rob, Rhys' secretary, places his plate down and arranges his cutlery before we can reply.

"Of course." Janet smiles.

I've not had a lot to do with Rhys or Rob, but I know the secretaries rave about what a ray of sunshine he is in their pod. He came with Rhys when he joined the firm, and I think he is the first male legal secretary we've had.

Both Rhys and Rob are extremely good-looking men, although I note Rob wears a ring. I don't think they're a couple, but they might be. My brother, Henry, is gay and hates it when women hit on him, presuming he's straight. Not that I want to hit on Rhys, but I can see a lot of women would. He's got that tall athletic thing happening with nicely styled blond hair that's longer on top. Today, he's clean-shaven, but I've seen him with stubble, too, and it's not a bad look on him. I think the most striking thing about him, apart from his square jaw, is his eyes. I've seen them look green and then hazel at other times. It probably helps that they're framed by glasses that really help set them off.

I may not have had a lot to do with Rhys, but I sure have noticed him, or at least my body has. I have my rules, though, and I won't act on any attraction. Instead, I'll look on from afar and pretend he's a Holly-wood heartthrob who would never notice me.

From what I've observed, Rhys can be very serious, but sometimes, he smiles, and his face lights up. I've seen him do this at the office when he's been watching someone do something that amuses him, like the time Janet dropped three files and, despite the papers being secured appropriately, she jumped up and down in her heeled shoes, her hands pumping up and down beside her. I think we all laughed at her, but seeing Rhys' reaction was something else.

"You've gone for the Moroccan tofu, too, I see, Valerie." Rhys pokes at his noodles with a fork, lifting them as if he hopes some meat will mysteriously appear underneath them.

"Please, just Val. I think I'm in trouble if my full name's used. And this is quite tasty. Of course, it would be tastier with a glass of red."

"Speaking my language." Rob has also chosen the tofu and vegetable option and nods in satisfaction as he takes his first bite. "Well, this is flavoursome at least."

"Look, I know we aren't the largest law firm in Brisbane by a long shot, but whose idea was the alcohol-free vegan fest?" It's not the food I'm complaining about, really, but the lack of alcohol is disturbing. "I mean, I thought we were going to a resort somewhere, and we could sit around and drink cocktails and get to know each other better." I sigh.

"Can we just blame Katherine?" One side of Rob's mouth lifts as he asks, and Rhys simply shakes his head. "Although, I know some of the newer folks amongst us are looking forward to getting to know everyone a little better, plus it means Rhys can't hide from us all."

A pink tinge spreads up Rhys's neck at Rob's words. I can't tell if he is naturally a shy person or if he is concerned Rob is going to spill things he doesn't want the rest of us to know. Whatever it is, I decide I'll get to know Rob a little better this weekend.

"Well, Val forgot *Twister*." Janet rolls her eyes. "Although, that may actually save us from needing some HR input, as she is extremely competitive."

"Am not," I cry. Okay, I totally am.

"Whatever you say, Valerie." Janet tucks into her dinner.

"Have you got your truths and lies sorted?" Rhys asks, and I look at him blankly, making him roll his eyes. "Did you read the information pack?"

"I think the email is in my to-read box, and I was going to do it tonight, but they confiscated my phone when I arrived." Rhys is a partner, and I hate to be shown up as the one person who hasn't done their homework. I don't dare mention that Katherine shoved a printout in my hand as I left the registration desk.

"Yes, well," he draws out with a sigh, "it said you need to prepare your two truths and a lie for one of the activities, and it mentioned no phones."

"Perhaps it's lucky I didn't read it then, because I might have got lost on my way here otherwise." I'm not sure if I'm trying to rile Rhys up, but it's fun just chatting with him. I don't think he knows how to take me, and I'm fine with that.

Our dinners finished, Rhys gathers our plates and goes to place them on the appropriate trolly, forbidding any help from us.

"He's quite shy." Rob leans into Janet and me as if he's telling us top secret information. "But once you get to know him, he's such a wonderful person. I mean, he's kind and generous and would do anything for those he cares about."

Rob's secret sharing is interrupted by Katherine again as she stands at the doorway to the room. "Okay, team." Katherine clasps her hands against her chin as if she's super excited about things. "Tonight is speed dating. It's time for you to get two minutes with a colleague to ask them anything. Questions can be work related or not. It's up to you, but remember, you're also trying to win two truths and a lie. Now, I've got the sheets here. Come and grab one and write your interesting facts down, but remember, one has to be a lie, and I'll pin them up in the conference room this evening so you can start deducing what your colleagues are pulling your legs with.

"Tomorrow, breakfast is at half-past eight. Rhys is going for a run at seven if anyone wants to join him, and I believe Melinda is offering yoga at the same time. I'll see you all in the conference room next door in fifteen minutes."

Yoga sounds interesting. It's something I've been waiting to try for a while. I know my bestie, Emily, did it during her pregnancy. It sounds better than a run, that's for sure.

Coming up with two truths and a lie isn't a challenge. As they say, truth can be stranger than fiction. I know Janet will know mine, but I'll also know hers, so we'll even each other out. I jot them down on the page, show them to Janet—who agrees they're good ones—and hand the form back to Katherine.

"Now, Katherine, you aren't suggesting dating colleagues here, I hope, because I don't date in the workplace." I smile as she sighs and tilts her head to the side, as if she thinks I'm an idiot. It's a look I'm well used to, and I know she gives it out of love and respect.

"It's a getting to know you weekend, Val. Speed dating was easier to say than speed getting to know you time or something. And we don't have non-fraternisation policies, what with two of the partners being married to each other. Now, which of these is the lie? It's the first one, no?"

"Actually, it's the third one." I shrug.

I head into the conference room where there are eighteen chairs arranged in two rows of nine. I see Melinda sitting and chatting with one of her paralegal colleagues and sit across from her. Everyone else files in, and the bell sounds to start our getting to know you rounds.

"So, yoga. Can you do it if you are totally uncoordinated like me?" I spit out.

"Absolutely." Melinda is measured in her reply, but I feel I need to be quick.

"Okay, I think I have some shorts I can wear, but I don't have any yoga pants. Problem?"

"No," she says sarcastically. "But if you read the information in the email—"

"Let's just assume I lost it." I raise my eyes and tilt my head back, only to see Melinda laughing for real now.

"No, you don't need to be coordinated. Anyone can do it, and I'll do some simple exercises with extensions for those of us who are used to them. There's no need to worry."

"Good. Did you have the noodles or the tofu?" I shoot out.

"Noodles, and they were delicious. I need to ask for the recipe. The mushrooms were so good."

"So, what do you do outside of work, apart from yoga?"

"I like to read, and I read smut, which shocks a lot of people." Melinda seems to take sharing this information in her stride.

"Me too," I let out excitedly. "As well as crime and thrillers. Have you read the latest TL Swan?"

"Day of release. Like, hello?" Melinda's voice raises as if everyone should have read it as soon as possible.

We carry on our talk about books until the bell rings, and we move to the next seat. I just go where I'm told, as Max has worked out a plan that will see everyone interact with everyone else.

I get Janet next, and we spend three minutes laughing as she impersonates several of our colleagues. She's so kind in the way she does it, too. Other people might take the piss and ham it up, but she shows just how lovely they are. Her impersonation of me forgetting something is spot on, even if I roll my eyes at her.

"Wait, no, is the retreat this weekend? It slipped my mind. I'll bring *Twister*." Janet does a decent impersonation of me, I have to admit.

"I had it in my diary, and I knew it was coming up. I just didn't realise it was this weekend," I reply, thinking back to our conversation in the tea room last Monday. "I'm not *that* forgetful."

"Two words, Val," she says, holding up two fingers. "Car registration."

"We're still not talking about that."

"You should have offered him a blowjob." She huffs out a breath.

"He was greying and was wearing a ring. You know I don't do married men."

The bell rings, and I spend three minutes quizzing Sarah-Jane, one of our new legal secretaries, why she isn't considering law school, seeing she has such an aptitude for what she does and loves a good argument. I think I've just about convinced her by the time the bell rings again. Max is next with her, and I tell him to keep trying to persuade her, which makes them both laugh.

Rhys takes a chair opposite me. "So, why family law?" he asks before he's even sat down.

"I loved the subject at uni, and I appreciate helping people get out of unpleasant situations," I say very matter-of-factly.

Rhys crosses his legs, so I do the same, except I also cross my arms across my chest.

"Why maritime law?" I ask him back.

"Because I love the sea."

Whereas I'm looking defensive with my arms crossed, he leans forward a bit, and I catch a whiff of his aftershave. It smells like the sea mixed with cloves and cinnamon. It's such a strange combination, but it's lovely in its uniqueness, and I can't help breathing in again to get another hit.

"So, you're anti-marriage then?" he asks, looking at me with his brow furrowed.

"I don't think so. I mean, I've got married brothers, and my parents are totally loved up after almost forty years, but yes, I've seen the one in three that end in disaster. We need to reconsider our notions of marriage if we want full equality. I mean, neither men nor women are property, and I've seen too many women simply become maids for men who can't be bothered lifting a finger." Rhys has really set me off on one of my rants. "Plus, who would put up with me? I mean, really? I'd forget the wedding was even on."

"See, I don't think you're that forgetful." Rhys taps his chin with his finger. "I think you take on everything yourself and have trouble trusting other people. I think—" Rhys doesn't get to finish what he thinks as the bell rings, and he is forced to move. He looks like he doesn't want to go, and I want to shoo the next person around him so he can stay for longer, but it's not in the spirit of the exercise.

His words leave me thinking, though. It's often easier to joke about things, but the truth is I don't have a great dating history. It's easy to find a guy who wants sex, but a guy who wants to be in an equal partnership and who shares my values... well, I might as well be looking for a unicorn. My brothers are awesome and have set the bar high for what I deserve in a partner. We had excellent role models in our parents, but even my sisters-in-law, who had shit examples of fathers, have built amazing family units.

Of all the conversations I have with colleagues—even though I've learnt some fascinating things about everything, from plant propagation to Australian ice-hockey leagues—it's my conversation with Rhys that stays with me. Even though I don't understand why, I want to know what he thinks. I want to know how he sees me, and I want to finish our conversation. Maybe he's also onto something, and deep down, I want what my brothers have. I want to be loved and cherished. Yes, I'd adore kids of my own. One day, perhaps, but not today. I have to look forward to a weekend where I'll survive on tofu and no alcohol first.

## 2

## Rhys

MAX HAS ALWAYS BEEN ONE OF MY MENTORS, ESPECIALLY SO after Uncle Derek died. He's encouraged me, and even though he knows little about maritime law, he's been there to suggest solutions when I need him. When he and Katherine offered me partner in their firm last year, I jumped at it. After four years of instability and simply sailing up and down the coast looking for work, I decided it was time to lay down some roots.

Sure, I still live on *Serenity*, my yacht, but I'm looking at moving into a house or even an apartment sometime this year. And yeah, 'yacht' possibly sounds pretentious, because it's really just a big sailing boat that has a cabin I can sleep in, a galley I can cook in, and a poor excuse for a bathroom. It's the closest I've come to living the carefree lifestyle of my parents, something I've always eschewed.

I'm not much of a speaker. Max argues that when I say something, it's something important. And yes, that makes it strange that I've made law my career. So, when I blurted out in a partners meeting soon after I arrived that I thought this team building weekend could be fun and a way for the newbies in the office to get to know everyone else a little better, Max and Katherine embraced the idea with open arms.

I didn't tell them that I had an ulterior motive and there's one colleague in particular I want to get to know. *Valerie Hartman.* She's so full of life. And she's gorgeous. Her short dark hair is styled in a pixie cut which, despite her taller frame, gives her an ethereal look. What really does me in though is her elfish face with round cheeks and those blue eyes that always have a glint to them. I've seen her at work on days when she's not going to court with no makeup on, and her face still shines. She doesn't need powders and potions to bring her face to life. It's always alive, and every time I see it, my heart skips a beat.

So, yeah, I've got a bit of a crush on Val. Rob recognises it. He's been my legal secretary for five years, and I think he's enjoyed having me around again instead of relying on video chats as I sailed up and down the coast while he stayed in Brisbane. No one in the office knows—I don't think—but he's also my brother-in-law, married to Myf, my outgoing, social sister.

It was Rob who steered us to Val's table for dinner. Watching her enjoy her meal with over-the-top facial expressions made me want to ignore my meal and just stare at her. Her moans and groans... well, they made my cock take notice. In the end, I had to look away and focus on my food, all but ignoring the surrounding conversation.

And then, at speed dating, well, I wished it was a date with Val. Three minutes was hardly enough time, and I would have loved longer, but the bell rang, and we both had to move on. Her rant about marriage made sense. I agree with every word, but she didn't let me get a word in, which actually suited me. I could listen to her all day, and I can only imagine what a force she is in the courtroom.

I've decided along the way that there are two groups of people who get into the law. There's the group who knows they'll charge by the fifteen-minute increment and make truckloads of money, and there are those, like Val, who do it to make the world a better place. I'd like to think I fall into the second category, too. Rob is always chastising me for not keeping track of my billable time, but really, if I can whip out a letter for someone that will save them thousands in fees, then why wouldn't I?

Uncle Derek was a mix of both kinds of lawyers, which worked out well for Myf and me, as we benefitted from an inheritance when he died.

If I can use some of it to provide free services to friends and neighbours at the marinas I moor at, then I at least feel like I'm paying it forward.

I've not slept well. The bed in my room at the resort is not the comfiest, and knowing I have a painting of Jesus with a glowing heart looking down at me is a little freaky. The curtains don't close properly, so every time I open my eyes, I see Him judging me. I spent hours reflecting on the concept of judgement from a higher being. Strange seeing I'd not been brought up to believe in such things. At 3 a.m., I removed the painting from the wall and placed it upside down on the desk.

When I finally nodded off, I dreamt of Val. Again. It's been a recurring theme for weeks now. This time, she was dressed in a gaudy white wedding gown with frills and lace bits that really didn't suit her. Her hair was longer and swept up against her head, held together with spray and pins that looked totally uncomfortable. What was worse, the brightness in her eyes had dulled because she was marrying me.

Gripping her arm, I was trying to tell her she didn't need to go through with it, but she simply kept patting her stomach as it started growing. I've never had sex without a condom I've supplied. I'm meticulous in their use. The thought I could actually impregnate her and use it as a trap is as likely as me becoming a standup comedian.

I finally give up on sleep and get out of bed, so I'm downstairs ten minutes early, waiting for those who want to join me on a run. I'm seriously hoping no one shows and I can go by myself and pound it out along the paths around the centre. I run almost every day. If I don't, my mind suffers. I'm hoping Val isn't a runner. The thought of her being near me and seeing her body move as she runs sends tingles to my groin, and an erection in running shorts is almost impossible to hide.

"Morning." Rob yawns as he appears through the door to the verandah where we're meeting. His hair is pointing in every direction, and he scratches his back as he holds his elbow behind him.

"Running?" I ask, trying not to sound too hopeful.

"Nah. Thought I'd try yoga. Make myself a little more flexible for Myf." Rob wiggles his eyebrows as he says this, knowing I hate to hear about my sister's sex life.

Val suddenly appears in baggy shorts with a singlet top. Her bra straps peek out from the thin straps. Seeing her feet are bare, I'm almost relieved she's here for yoga. I can't look her in the eye for fear she'll see the desire hiding there.

I'm glad when the big hand gets to the top of the hour, and no one is here to run with me. Melinda has most of the office, save Max and Katherine, who want to test their flexibility. I think it's best I leave them to it.

Setting out through the car park, I turn right and find a path that leads into bushland. The map of the site shows that most tracks loop around and find their way back to the main building. Not knowing the path, I don't keep my usual pace but can get into the rhythm that sees my feet fall as they need to and my arms pump by my side.

There's no music, seeing I don't have access to my phone, but the birds serenade me with their morning melodies, save for a kookaburra who simply wants to laugh at me. He's not the first bird to think I'm a bit of a joke. I waited months for Stacey Shilling to decide she was ready to take our high school relationship to the next level. There was no way I was going to pressure her. We finally had sex together for the first time just after our high school graduation. I know my parents thought we'd been at it for months.

I thought she was the one, but she made it clear she, too, thought I was a bit of a joke. Her rejection has always stung, and even thinking of this memory years later makes me wonder if she was right.

There have been a few other women, but most have only stuck around once they realise I received an inheritance from my uncle and have a well-paying job. I don't mind spoiling partners with perfumes and jewellery, but I prefer to do it on my terms, rather than having demands made of me.

I've never dated a colleague. Throughout law school, I focused on my studies rather than parties or getting laid. Sure, it was boring, but I have a desire to succeed in everything I do. I'm a planner. Well, I try to be. It's hard being thirty-four and having not met goals. I thought I'd be a dad by now. I thought I would have found my person. But it hasn't happened.

As I come around a bend, I realise I must be near the main hall, as I can hear laughter from the yoga group.

"I'm sorry, I'm sorry. It's from growing up with brothers." Val's laughter is as bright as the rest of her. "But you have to admit, a fart is always funny."

Hearing her so relaxed and laughing like this makes my heart swell. I've looked at Val from afar, but it's these glimpses I'm getting this weekend that are doing nothing to quell the growing desire I feel for her.

My path comes out the other side of the building, and I eye where I can head to next, nowhere near done with my run yet. Max and Katherine are sitting together drinking their morning cuppas on the verandah. I love that they have each other. They support one another and are each other's biggest cheerleaders. Derek was close to them, too. He never married. Well, he was married to his job.

As much as I love my job, I want something more, someone more. I need to use this weekend to get to know Val better and see if perhaps there is something there we can explore. Fuck, I sound clinical. I sound like a real desperado. Maybe I am. I don't know what it is this woman holds over me, but I'm just drawn to her, and I need to work out what to do about it. All I know is that it feels more than a physical pull that makes me believe that Val and I could have something special, something more than the physical release I've experienced with women in the past.

I try not to think about my parents' relationship. I know it suits them, and they've been together for almost forty years, but it's not the kind of relationship I'm looking for. The way they practice free love is not for me. I'd love to think that one day I'll have a piece of paper that says I'm legally married to someone, but I also believe that a commitment without vows and rings and pieces of paper can be just as strong. Despite my parents' beliefs, I've always believed in monogamy. They think it's great that I'm not married and am living a free life. Not in the way they think, though.

After forty-five minutes of exploring different paths, I head back to my room for a shower. As I bound up the steps and along the corridor towards my room, I see Val leaving the bathrooms, a towel wrapped around her as she scurries for her room.

"Sorry, I forgot to take my clothes, but hey, I remembered a towel, right?" she jokes as she passes me.

"Morning," I reply and instantly chastise myself. What a fucking innocuous thing to say. Why can't I flirt a little, tell her clothes are overrated? Except I'm not that guy. I don't like making people feel uncomfortable, knowing I'm the one who usually feels that way.

Val rushes past me, and I smell the citrus from her bath products. It's intoxicating. I want to hold her close and breathe her in.

"You're going to be late for breakfast." Rob greets me as he leaves his room and I get to my door. "Looking extra sweaty. You should have done yoga."

There's no way I could have gotten through yoga with Val in the same vicinity. The rest of this weekend is going to be bloody hard enough as it is. I need to suck it up and find a way to talk to her and get to know her better.

"It's okay, you're safe. Just look ahead at the trees. Can you see the cockatoos over there?" I point towards a eucalypt that has a swarm of birds sitting in its canopy. High ropes have never bothered me, but Janet is not as convinced.

"I should have gone with Val and done the stupid orienteering." Janet's legs are shaking, and she is suspended halfway between ledges, the ropes swaying as she tries to remain still.

"Nah, Val should have come and done this with you." I sound calm. Heights don't scare me at all. "Just inch your foot towards the next ledge. Nice and slow." Janet does this, the ropes swaying as her foot moves. "You've got this. You're almost there."

Janet is moving slowly, and she's going to make it. I still don't know why I'm the one coaching her while the instructor is still on the ground.

"Tell me about how you and your partner met."

Janet chuckles, but she's still moving, albeit really slowly. "Penny came to Brisbane from Cassowary Point. Her dad owns hotels up there and worked with a friend of Val's parents. They heard she was coming down here and said she could move into the apartment I shared with Val. The rest is history, I suppose."

The irony that Janet almost falls as her foot hits the safety of the platform between the ropes is not lost on me, but she is on a solid ledge at our next safe point. This is the hardest of the hurdles we are facing on the course, slacker ropes with only one for hands and one for feet. The ladders and thicker taut ropes with handles on either side were much easier.

I indicate to the instructor below that I'm ready to go and make a quick pace of the section.

"Show off." Janet shakes her head, but she has a smile on her face.

"I'm used to ropes and suspension," I say, causing Janet to wiggle her eyebrows suggestively.

"Can't wait to spread that around the office."

It's only then I realise what I've said. "I'm a sailor. I'm not into tying up women or being tied up myself."

I know I'm red. I wish the ground would open up, and it's almost tempting to jump off here and run away.

We reach the last section, and Janet makes it look easy. I suspect she's still laughing at me. The cockatoos we saw in the tree swarm above us, off to look for the next place to perch. Despite the no alcohol rule and the uncomfortable beds, it's a beautiful place to escape to.

Janet climbs down the ladder from our last ledge, and I follow suit. I'd rather have abseiled down, but I don't want to show off. We're the last ones to finish, but a few of our colleagues have stayed behind to cheer us on.

"That was amazing, Janet. You rocked that." One of the secretaries throws her arms around her for a hug. Others pat her on the shoulder.

"Well done, mate." The guy in charge of the course pats me on the shoulder as I shimmy out of my harness. "I prefer it on these team building things for colleagues to encourage each other. You did well with her up there."

It was good to hear this from the person running the high ropes, but it would also have been good to hear it from my colleagues. I'm a junior partner. Few make partner before they're thirty-five. Not being around the office much also puts me at a disadvantage. I should make more of an effort to get in there, but a lot of my business is from others who live at the wharf, and it seems counterintuitive to make them come into the office when we can meet for a drink nearby.

I make my way towards the main building. We have an hour before dinner, and I'm in desperate need of some alone time to recharge. Being amongst people is not my idea of relaxation.

"Hey, Rhys," Janet calls from ahead of me where she is walking with our colleagues. "I owe you a beer for saving me up there. Wish we could grab one tonight, but alas... Seriously though, you were amazing."

My cheeks flush at hearing these words in front of my colleagues.

"What did Rhys do now?" Katherine appears from inside the door.

"He saved me on the high ropes. I will not do that again, even if I managed to finish it. How was orienteering?"

"We lost Val." Katherine chuckles, but my chest seizes.

"Did you find her?" I blurt out, my eyes wide and my heart racing.

"Yes." Katherine shakes her head. "There'll be no lawsuits against us. Don't stress."

I wasn't worried about Val suing us. I was more concerned about her being lost and alone.

"Here she is, all safe and sound." Katherine wraps her arm around Val's waist, and Val places her head on her boss's shoulder. I wish she was doing this to me.

"How did you get lost?" Janet's shoulders shake as she tries to withhold her laughter.

"I saw an echidna and followed it, except then I forgot which way I was meant to be going, but then it didn't matter, as I found a second echidna, and they were a pair, and I think I got to see an echidna mating dance, well, not dance, but they were clearly hot for each other."

"Oh, yeah?" Janet bumps hips with Val, her arms in the air.

I want to say something smart or witty. I want to make a comment that I need to take lessons from these echidnas, but I'm mute, struck dumb with nothing to say. Story of my life.

I DIDN'T GET to sit with Val at dinner. Melinda and Sandra dragged Rob and me to their table. Both are fun women who spent the time talking about how they were enjoying a weekend away from their husbands. Melinda has young children at home and is concerned her husband won't be able to cope without her. It made me angry when she talked about Duane having no idea how to use the washing machine or what their kids eat for breakfast.

How women put up with that is beyond me. My parents may be alternative, but they took an interest in Myf and me. I knew how to use a washing machine from about ten years old, and I knew to pump the grey water into the garden. Dad's only ever done odd jobs, and it was common for him to be home after school preparing dinner. Hearing about Melinda and Duane makes me wonder how common this is.

Myf and Rob almost broke up over Rob expecting specific gendered roles. It was before he became my legal secretary. I spent an evening talking to him over a pint and was amazed that he didn't consider anything other than the patriarchal bullshit he'd been exposed to growing up.

"Remember, Katherine and Val will take him to the cleaners when you finally decide to leave him." Sandra is angry for her colleague and friend, too.

"I know, but..." Melinda shakes her head as her thoughts trail off.

"How did you meet?" Rob asks as he takes a bite of his pasta dish. I've chosen the chickpea curry and am amazed at how much flavour they've packed in.

"He was dared to come to my yoga class, and we went out for a drink afterwards. The rest is history."

"So, you've always taught yoga?" I ask as I take a sip of the sparkling water that's been provided. A beer would be a better bet right now.

"I used to have my own studio." Melinda shrugs. "I sold it when we got married so we could put a deposit on a house."

"And you no longer teach?"

"Oh, god no." Melinda almost chokes on her curry. "Duane would have a fit if he thought people were looking at me in my yoga gear."

"Hmm." I frown.

"Being a legal secretary is acceptable." Melinda shrugs, and I wonder if she can read my thoughts. "And when I started, there weren't many younger men around the firm. That was also acceptable to Duane."

"So, you're working in a job that's not your first choice and still doing everything at home?" Rob places his spoon and fork together on his plate and drops his serviette on top. "Sounds like he needs more than a weekend with your kids. Sounds like he needs to start being a father."

"He loves them. He really does." Melinda bites her lower lip.

I hope we've given her food for thought. Rob's great at how he reacts, but I really just sat there like a stunned mullet. I know she has to be the one to make the decision to leave, but it must be hard with young kids at home.

Excusing myself from the table, I once again grab the plates and scrape them, placing them in the plastic racks that will make their way through the dishwasher later. At least we don't have kitchen duty.

Our table was one of the last to finish, and I find almost everyone else is in the conference room, games set up at different stations. My eyes are drawn to Val, who has five other colleagues around her as they set up *Monopoly*. Looks like that table's full.

Katherine and Max have set up cards.

"I'm guessing it's not *Go Fish* you're playing?" I ask as I sit and lean against the back of a chair.

"Sandra and Ian were planning on joining us for *Bridge*. Do you play?" Katherine shuffles the cards without looking at them. It seems something she's comfortable doing.

"No, but I'm sure I'll find something." I smile. "Enjoy."

Rob has joined the group playing *Risk*, a game I've played before. I don't want to be seen as always doing things with Rob, though. Sure, it's comfortable, but I need to break out of my comfort zone. In the end, I join Janet and two other lawyers who are setting up *Scrabble*. I like Janet. She's a straight shooter and appears extremely competent in her field of contract law. Donny is our tax law specialist, and Cheng is known as a ball breaker when it comes to employment law. I heard him speak at a conference a couple of years ago about being born in Australia and growing up here and people having preconceived notions about him because he uses his non-Anglo name.

We draw our tiles, and I have very little to work with. The closest letter to A I have is an E. Janet does a dance as she proclaims she drew a blank tile and an A, and we all agree she will start. I can see why she's happy, as she places the blank tile and works backwards to reveal the word 'jazz'.

I'm last to play in our four and am glad I can add a Y to the end of Janet's word. There's no added value to the tile, but still, I'm just glad I could create a word with my terrible bunch of letters.

We continue our game, and I'm able to add on here and there, but the tile gods aren't on my side. After several rounds, though, things fall into place, and I place 'quaky' with the help of some other letters already on the board.

We're all lawyers and have a fairly wide vocabulary, but I spent hours one summer reading my uncle's *Scrabble* dictionary and remember a lot of the silly little words that can score decent points. Some words make us laugh, and it's fun getting to know Donny and Cheng better. Donny tells stories about his partner of twenty-six years and his work as a train driver, and Cheng boasts about helping the train driver's union get a decent pay rise for their members recently.

"And what about you, Rhys?" Donny asks as he places down letters to form 'askew' using a double word square on the w. There's no chance I'll win tonight, but I'm having fun. "You got a partner?"

"Not at the moment, no." I end up adding an S to an existing word on the board for a few points. "I've been itinerant for the last few years, but one of the reasons I came back here is because I want to settle down, I think."

"I've got a niece who's single," Donny says as he rearranges tiles on his holder.

I don't want to be set up. Blind dates are the worst. There's the expectation that others think you'll be great together, but I'm usually so nervous I make a fool of myself or say something that is taken the wrong way.

"We'll see," I reply as Janet swaps from tiles in the bag. It's rather nice to see she can't play anything either.

I get Cheng talking about his family and am pleased when he says he hates leaving everything for his wife to do all weekend, but he's promised her he'll cook dinner Sunday night when he's back.

We finish our game with me bringing up the rear, but it is closer than I thought it would be. The *Bridge* crew have headed to bed and the *Risk* players are packing up. It's the *Monopoly* crew who are still playing. I look over to see Val smile and laugh, doing a little dance as someone lands on one of her properties. Melinda loudly claims she's out and hands her cards to Val, who looks like she now owns half the board, and they all agree she's the winner.

While it's been nice to get to know some of the team, it's Saturday night, and I'm no closer to getting to know Val. Perhaps I should get up early tomorrow and go for a run before joining them for yoga. I know I need sleep, though, and I trudge up the stairs with Rob, who proudly claims he smashed everyone at *Risk*, even though there's no one to dispute his claims.

"Talk to her, mate." He nudges me with his shoulder as we walk along the corridor, knowing how I feel about Val.

"I know, I know."

# 3

# Val

I'D FORGOTTEN HOW MUCH FUN *MONOPOLY* IS, ESPECIALLY with people who aren't members of my family. Last time I played at home, Boyd and Emily teamed up and annihilated me. *Some best friend she is.* Last night, I won fair and square. Well, with a lot of luck and dice rolls going my way.

For years, I've worked with these people, but I don't know them very well. I'm always busy at work. I try to work smarter, not harder, but it often means I'll work through my lunch break, shovelling a sandwich in my mouth as I focus on the file I need to have completed for the afternoon.

It's clear how little I know about my colleagues when I come across their 'Two truths and a lie' submissions. Is Sandra's husband her high school sweetheart, or is it that she wins prizes in the state show for her needlepoint? I've never seen her do crafty things, but it wouldn't surprise me. In the end, I decide the lie is that she wanted to name her firstborn son Leopold after her father, but her husband was having none of it.

This morning I'd done yoga again, and Melinda has lined me up with a class near the office that I'm planning on trying. We then had a talk from Katherine and Max about things that were happening around the office. None of it is groundbreaking, but it was nice to hear it from the horse's mouth, so to speak, rather than in an email.

Lunch was a vegan barbecue, and whilst I won't be rushing out to buy meat-free sausages, the accompanying salads were delicious.

"Hmm, Val, I can't believe any of these are true. They all seem so farfetched." Rhys is looking studiously at my 'Two truths and a lie' contribution, which was hung next to his. "I find it hard to believe that both your parents are doctors, your brothers are all doctors, and their partners are all doctors. Surely, there must be some diversity in there?"

"I will neither confirm nor deny." I hold my hands behind my back, interested to see where his surmising was going.

"I do like this one, and I suspect it has to be true, because it is the least incredulous of the lot. You probably live with a cat and three goldfish in a purpose-built condo overlooking the ocean."

"I will not give you any hints. My three options have even baffled."

This was the most we had ever talked together, and I could see Rhys was shy, just as Rob had warned me. There was also something else about him though, a thought process that saw him analyse my truths and lies and come at them from both sides of what could be argued. It was what probably made him an amazing lawyer.

"Well, I doubt that both of your parents were born one day either side of Valentine's Day, married on Valentine's Day, all their children are February babies, and they are both Valentine's mad, holding a Valentine's party each year."

I knew I was going to baffle most people with my facts.

"I will admit yours are fairly straightforward, Mr Partner." I turned to him and crossed an arm across my chest, a finger tapping at my chin. "I'm pretty sure you do live on a boat, yet it may not be called *Serenity,* because that seems too calm almost. I'm willing to believe you have been married and divorced, however, you do not strike me as being someone who was raised by hippies—you're too refined for that. I suspect your father at least is in the law and you've lived a life of privilege."

"Well, we'll find out soon enough." Rhys smiles. His shoulders slump as Katherine appears at the front of the room. "Look, they're trying to gather us together again already."

I find Janet, and we sit in the large circle that has been set up for the morning. I have to admit, it has not been all bad, and whilst it was terrifying at first to check our phones in as we arrived, being unplugged had been quite pleasant and helped me, at least, be in the moment.

"Thanks, team. Let's bring it in one last time." Katherine's smile is infectious, and I love looking around the room and seeing my colleagues so happy and relaxed. "I think we can all agree that it has been a productive weekend. We had some changes last year with some long-serving staff moving on or retiring and some new staff joining us, especially Rhys Evans as a partner, and it would seem that although Max assured me it would be Rhys who would be the most elusive in 'Two truths and a lie', he has just been pipped at the post by Ms Valerie Hartman, who has baffled us the most, and considering you've been with us, what, five years now?"

"About that, Katherine, yes, but I'm still not prepared to say which was the lie." I laugh. Although, I was amazed I had fooled so many of my colleagues and wondered which they thought most likely to be fictional, it also made me realise how I needed to socialize more with people at work.

Melinda and Sandra reach over and pat me on the knee.

Soon, we were gathering our mobile phones and packing the last things into our cars. The music that had been our soundtrack on the way up here was turned down as Janet started the vehicle.

"Are you right to go out tonight or would you rather spend the evening with Penny alone?" I asked as we turned out of the retreat centre.

"Would you mind? I mean, without phones and contact and all, I missed her so much." Janet bites her lip as she sneaks a quick glance at me. It's almost sickening how wonderful the two of them are together, and this did not surprise me in the least.

"Not at all. I must admit, I am feeling a little perkier after all the healthy food, and one more night of it won't hurt me." I press my head back against the rest of my seat and smile at the memories of the weekend. "Melinda's even found a yoga class for me tomorrow evening. I hope I won't fart again," I declare playfully.

As we drive, I power on my phone and listen to my voicemail messages, all from my family. Mum reminds me the Valentine's gala is coming up. It's hardly something I'd forget. Henry, my middle brother —who, like his partner Ken, is a psychiatrist—had called from a trivia night, suspecting I would know the answer to a question on constitutional law. Emily rang just to see how I was, even though I heard baby Issy in the background crying. Finally, Giles, my oldest brother—who is also a cardiologist like my parents—had rung to remind me he'd be in the city this week and wanted to confirm dinner.

"All good?" Janet asks as I hang up.

"Yeah." I sigh. "It's Mum's and Dad's birthdays and their fortieth wedding anniversary this Valentine's, and they've organised another huge gala to raise money for the cardiac department at their hospital. They hold a party every year and this gala every five. It's, like, bigger than *Ben Hur*. Mum, Dad, Boyd, and Emily will all be setting me up with guys they think are perfect for me—and of course, all of them will be doctors—and will hint, not too subtly, that it's time to settle down."

"Well, why don't you get in first and tell them you're bringing someone?" Janet is all matter-of-fact as she takes the bends in the road down the hill.

"Like who? My last relationship was a disaster, but luckily, none of them met Craig. I'm hardly able to just take one of the guys I pick up home to Mum and Dad, am I?"

My last few years of dating have been a mess. I joke that I only give a guy one chance to give me an orgasm and then I move on, but even the ones who have managed to help me come have been losers after a few dates.

"Well, why don't you ask someone like Rhys? I mean, he's a partner, so that would be good in your parents' eyes. He's bloody hot, even for a dyke like me, and, as far as I know, he's single. He'd be the perfect pretend boyfriend."

I wonder to myself if Janet has a point. I adore my family, but I'm definitely the black sheep. When I told Mum and Dad that I was going to study law, they told me that at least I could still marry a doctor. I've never been sure if they were a hundred percent serious, but it's always been implied. I hadn't spent Christmas with my family, knowing I would spend Valentine's Day at home, and I know deep down, I miss them all terribly.

After Janet dropped me at home, a humble worker's cottage that was so far away from the modern condo Janet and Penny lived in, I decide to try some of Janet's advice and call home.

"Hey, Mum. I'm just home from a team building weekend. How could you begin to think I could forget about Valentine's? Yes, it is in my diary. Well, I'm sure he is, but I'm sort of seeing someone. I mean, no, it's early days and all, but he's just lovely. No, Mum, no, I really don't want to... Mum, as I said, it's early days... Okay, I'll ask him, but he's probably going to be busy. Gee, thanks Mum, you think I'm that desperate I'd invent a boyfriend? Thanks a lot."

Mum was married at twenty-three and had had three sons by her thirtieth. I could never work out if I was an 'oops' or if I had been carefully planned when I came along a few years later as the long-awaited girl.

I know my family wants me to experience the happiness they've all found, but I wonder if they realise what pressure they're placing on me.

Perhaps Janet is right and I need to ask Rhys if he'll pretend to date me, just for the weekend. It's not like he'd have to attend. We could pretend he has another event on and just FaceTime or call each other or something.

Maybe her plan might just work.

I MEET Giles for dinner on Thursday evening as planned, alone, despite him asking to meet my new 'beau'. I'm not surprised Mum has been talking to my siblings. Giles is nine years older than me and has always looked out for me, despite our age difference. He met Bridget at medical school, and the two have been married for almost fifteen years. Their daughters, Millicent and Amelia, are growing into beautiful young women, and I love it when they fly down to spend time with me in the school holidays.

Once or twice a year, Giles also makes his way down here, and we dine together. Usually, he spends the time convincing me to retrain as a doctor, but lately, he's been all about marrying me off to a doctor. It's not going to happen.

"How are the girls?" I ask as I sit at our outside table overlooking the river. Despite the evening traffic, I don't mind coming into town to meet up with him.

"Yeah, good." A large grin sneaks across his face. "They both wanted to come down with me this week and see you, but Millie's doing swim camp, and Mia's insistent that she needs to practice for her piano exam, which isn't until July, mind you."

"And Bridget?" I peruse my menu, but I don't miss the way my brother's smile grows and his shoulders roll back.

"She's amazing."

He doesn't elaborate, but he doesn't need to. Bridget is great at everything she does. She's an amazing doctor, a phenomenal mother, and an integral part of our family. She's a no bullshit kind of woman and keeps us on our toes. Plus, she is the one who chastises my brothers for trying to set me up. I first met her when I was a teenager, and she's always been someone I respect. If only I was as organised as she is. One day I'll make a to-do list and not lose it before I've crossed anything off it.

"I flew down to shadow a colleague for a week as we try to finalise the design on the new stents we have been developing. But you don't want me to talk shop, do you?" Giles picks at a thick slice of bread they placed in front of us after we ordered.

"That's why you're my favourite big brother." I smirk as I take a sip of my wine. It's the first glass I've had since before the retreat.

"You say that to Henry and Boyd, too." Giles huffs and rolls his eyes.

"Yeah, maybe I do. So, what are we going to get Mum and Dad for their anniversary?"

That's the best thing about being the youngest in the family. No one expects me to organise anything. I turn up and do my bit. To be honest, I haven't thought about any ideas for gifts for my parents.

I think back to the last gala ball and how it was almost a disaster. Emily was convinced she'd never have a baby and had told Boyd she wanted a divorce so he could find someone else. He refused, of course. They agreed to try IVF again, but I know neither of them thought it would work. Emily is the first to chastise me when I suggest Issy is a blessing, telling me all children are, but knowing how long it took for her to join our family makes her that little more special in my eyes.

"Bee and I thought we could send them away for a week to an island or something." Giles brushes the crumbs off his hands as he sits back in his chair.

"That sounds ideal, and Mum would love that." I lean forward, thinking of all the different places they could go off the Queensland coast.

"Boyd reckons we get them a selection of sex toys, but I reckon he's got blue balls with the baby and all." I'm always surprised Giles' eyes aren't more defined, what with all the eye rolling he does.

"Issy's almost six months. It may have become less frequent, but surely... I mean, Emily would be gagging for it more than him, I reckon, and he's got the Hartman sex drive gene. What about Henry and Ken?" I make a mental note to check in with Emily soon. We've texted almost every day, but we haven't found a suitable time to talk.

"They like the idea of a holiday for them. Hen also suggested some professional family photos, which sound nice, too."

"Yeah, whatever. Just tell me how much I owe." The waiter places my bowl of seafood pasta in front of me, the rich tomato and garlic aromas hitting my nostrils and causing me to inhale deeply.

I tell Giles a bit about our weekend team building exercise, and he tells me that he can't imagine that happening in the hospital, partially because they would need people around to care for their patients. It reminds me again why I'm grateful I didn't go into medicine.

I knew medicine was expected of me, not necessarily by Mum and Dad, but more by Giles and, to a lesser extent, Henry. Boyd was stuck on impressing Emily from before she recognised boys existed to worry too much about my career choices, but Giles assumed I'd want to become a doctor. He decided I'd be a great cardiologist like him, Mum, and Dad. I mean, I love hearts, and I find them fascinating, but I think I'm more about the emotions rather than the way the valves and stuff work.

Early in high school, I discovered debating. I'd always loved reading; throw in a good argument, and a life in law seemed like an ideal career pathway. Giles still insists I'd be a great doctor, but I'll gladly leave medicine for my brothers and their partners.

"So, tell me about this new bloke of yours. Mum seems excited." Giles lifts his fork above his head, trying to break the string of cheese that is joined to the morsel on the tines and the rest of the dinner on his plate.

"It's just a guy from work. There's probably nothing in it, really." I shrug. I haven't spoken to Rhys yet, and I don't even know if he's up for it.

"You could start a new branch of the family. What's his surname? You know Hartman and whoever, partners in law or at law or whatever you legal eagles say." This is probably the first time Giles hasn't insisted I marry a doctor, and I see it as a step in the right direction.

"I'm not telling." I laugh as I drain my wine glass.

"Well, Boyd's got a surgeon lined up for you. He's got an enormous nose." And here it is.

"Is that code for he's hung?" I smirk, knowing the once self-proclaimed man-whore now hates talking about sex with his baby sister.

"Valerie." Giles drops his fork on the plate and looks around to make sure people aren't staring at us.

"Well, my brothers have all got small noses, and Emily has commented..." I trail off, my eyes wide and blinking rapidly.

"Oh my god. What has she said?" He places his hand on his forehead and rubs.

"I'm not sure about you or Henry, but apparently Boyd is hung like a fucking donkey."

Giles says nothing for a while, simply finishing his dinner. I love making him feel uncomfortable like this. Sometimes, I wonder if he still sees me as the baby sister and hasn't comprehended that I'm a grown-up woman now and have been for some years.

He orders dessert, and I sit back and sip my water.

"It will be good to have us all together again," Giles says, smiling. "You're flying up on Thursday, right?"

"Yeah, Thursday lunchtime, out Monday evening." I check my calendar on my phone and confirm the times. If it isn't in my calendar, it won't happen.

"You really should see if that fellow of yours could join us. We'd all like to meet him. I mean, it's been years since you've even mentioned a man in your life."

My brother has a point, but given the divorce statistics I'm reminded of every day, I'll leave the happy families to them.

EMILY

How was dinner with Giles?

I didn't tell him he's got some grey hair popping up.

EMILY

Don't worry, Bridget reminds him every day that his body is breaking down.

How's Issy?

THAT's the joy of texting my best friend. She can leave me hanging, and I know she'll come back when she can. Issy seems to be a placid baby, but she still wakes at night for a feed. I love the idea of babies, but I think I love the idea of sleep more. Henry and Ken talked babies a few years back, but I suspect with Emily and Boyd's infertility struggles, they put things on the back burner for a bit. It's always amazed me that Giles and Bridget stuck with only two kids. I imagined them having a much larger family.

People probably imagined me having a large family too, but I'm about to hit thirty with no prospects of a partner in sight, and I've probably left it a bit late.

EMILY

FML. She has a tiny belly; I get that, and I know I have to feed her more often, but I swear, those bowels must be huge. She can go days without a shit and then explode everywhere. It went all up her back and over me and then Rooster came in and started licking at it, causing me to almost vomit.

I can't stop laughing at Emily's text. Rooster is their dog, who seems more protective of Issy than anyone else. Emily isn't usually one to swear, either, and I wonder how much sleep she is missing out on. I wish I was up there helping her. I feel pretty useless being so far away. When we were growing up, we talked about having kids together and them playing and having sleepovers and running amok at family events.

There's no way I can move home without a partner, though. My family would have me on blind dates every night of the week and twice on Saturdays until I settled for someone. I don't want to settle. I want to find someone who challenges me and wants me for me. Life as a single mother isn't for me. I could find some sperm at a bank somewhere, but I know I'll need a village around me. I'll forget where I left the baby, let alone if I need to feed it, and I can see myself leaving home without all the necessities a baby requires.

> You're not selling motherhood to me.

EMILY

> It's amazing. I mean, are you free for a chat?

I look at my calendar. I have a client due any minute.

> Sorry. Client due. Tonight?

EMILY

> Lock it in.

A pop-up on my computer screen alerts me to my client's arrival. We've been hoping to avoid heading to court, but it appears the father is being a prick. At least the bastard put in writing that he's taking her to court so there won't be as much money for her to get in the property settlement. It means she should be able to claim costs from him, too, when the whole shit show is over. That he's making her go through with a trial knowing he doesn't see his kids when it's currently arranged, sends them back to their mother early, and the kids hate spending time with him frustrates me, but it is what it is, and I need to ensure the best for my client.

It's no wonder I'm wary of men when I'm often confronted with situations like these. Sure, I've represented some great fathers who've had wives try to screw them over, but they've been in the minority.

After work, as I wander to my car, I text Emily, asking if she's free to chat. I barely get the car door open before my phone rings.

"Hold on," I laugh. "Let me switch on the car and make sure you're on Bluetooth."

I throw my bag on the passenger seat and swear when things go flying.

"You okay?" Emily chuckles.

"Yeah." I sigh as I start to put things back in my bag. "I just found my old pair of sunnies that I thought I'd lost. They were under the seat. Must have fallen here the last time my bag went flying. Anyway. How are you?"

"You know." Emily tries to sound upbeat, but I hear the tiredness in her voice.

"Issy still not sleeping?" I ask as I turn on the car and pull out of the car park onto the main road.

"She's getting better, I suppose." My best friend sounds dejected, and I'm not really sure what to say. "I just..." Emily sighs. "I feel like I should be loving every second of it, especially after what we've been through, but I'm getting a little bored. I mean, I'm playing a lot of piano, but even that's not doing much for me."

"So, what about going back to work a day a week or something?" I ask, as I'm stuck in traffic. I should have stayed at work for another hour to avoid it. So much for me trying to create more of a balance.

"I'd like that."

"I'm sure your mum would look after Issy for a day, plus your Nonna would love it," I add, choosing not to beep my horn at the idiot who just cut in front of me.

"Yeah, but Boyd said that he'd take a day off, but he's so close to becoming a consultant. Plus—" Emily stops abruptly as I hear Boyd sing out that he's home. Rooster is no guard dog. "I'm on the phone with your sister."

"Hey, stinky," Boyd sings out, using my childhood nickname that I pretend to hate but secretly love. "How's my gorgeous Issybum? Look at you sucking at those amazing tits."

"Boyd," Emily almost screams down the phone as I assume my brother kisses her.

"I'm going to leave you to play happy families. Talk soon, okay?" I try to sound upbeat, but there's a tinge of sadness in my tone.

I've dreamt of a life they've made together, and I don't think it's going to be for me. I'll help people get out of their awful marriages and probably won't get into one myself. Emily and Boyd had to pivot when they had trouble conceiving, and I kept telling them they didn't know what the future held. It may be the same for me. Prince Charming might be ready to come and ride by my side as we save the world together, but I know it's unlikely.

# 4

# Rhys

My parents have never made me feel like I'm a disappointment, but I know that being a lawyer is the last thing they would have expected from me. I grew up being indoctrinated that capitalism is evil and free love will create peace. My sister and I were home-schooled for a while before being sent to an alternate school. Rhys seemed like a pretty ordinary name compared to Sunshine, Rainbeau, Blossom, River, and Logg—yes, with the double G.

I'm disappointed in myself, though. I wanted a team building weekend where I could get to know all my colleagues better, and the one I really wanted to get to know more about, well... I was too chickenshit to approach her like I dreamt of. Perhaps I should have done yoga, but then I would have had everyone else in the office watching me make a fool of myself.

I've spent more time in the office this week, wanting to just bump into her and have a conversation, but it didn't pan out. Maybe if I went to her office and had a chat, it might be different, but the thought of that has me breaking out in a cold sweat.

As I saw her leave on Friday, I followed her, thinking I could ask her for a drink or something. But no, she was on the phone, no doubt setting up a date with someone else. The smile on her face as she answered the call was radiant, her joy palpable. The effect she has on me... I've never felt like this about a woman before. It seems every night, and then again every morning, I jack off thinking about her, wondering what it would feel like to be inside her. My hand is hardly a substitute, but I make do.

Trying to stop my obsessional thoughts about her, I've taken *Serenity* out to throw a line or two in the water and see if I can catch some dinner. I'm heading to Myf and Rob's later, and I know they'll appreciate a fish or two. I pull out the latest book I'm reading: a thriller about a double agent. Poor guy's got himself in an absolute pickle, and I can't imagine how he's going to get out of it. I know he does, though, because there are three more books in the series, so I want to read on, but my mind keeps drifting to Valerie Hartman.

I'm not the sort of person who simply waltzes up to someone and asks them out. Usually, I have to know if the woman is interested. I know I'm a good-looking guy. I've had women approach me just because they like the way I look. Most haven't been interested in me enjoying reading or fishing. Some wanted a trip out on *Serenity* just so they could be seen at the marina and show off their string bikinis.

I've had a fair amount of sex, but whilst I've ensured my partners have been satisfied, at the end of the day, I haven't experienced total satisfaction, not the type I've dreamt about or that which is depicted in romance novels. See, I'm a wide reader, and there are some amazing books out there about true love, or what I imagine true love to be.

There's a tug on one of my lines, and I reel in a magnificent-looking threadfin salmon. That's dinner sorted. Somehow, the bait from my other line has disappeared, no doubt nibbled off by something that wasn't ready to be caught. At least I gave them an easy meal.

There's not a lot of wind, so I motor back to the marina, nodding at folks along the way—happy families out for a weekend sail, couples enjoying the sunshine. One vessel has a woman sunbathing topless on the stern, but she does nothing for me. I know the guy she's with, and he'll have a different woman tomorrow. That's not what I want, though. I want more. I want Valerie Hartman.

"I BROUGHT DINNER." I slide the cooler to Myf as Rob greets me with a bear hug. It made me laugh when people at work assumed Rob and I were together. He's a good-looking man, but I've never been tempted by men. It might be easier if I was, then I wouldn't be spending so much time lusting after my colleague who doesn't even notice me.

"Legend." Myf embraces me, and I twirl her around as I lift her from the floor. With a head full of dreadlocks and several piercings on her face, she could still fit into our parents' world, but her personality is a little more conventional, like mine, minus the shyness.

We've always been close. Myf followed me to Brisbane to study to become a nurse and then a midwife. I know she and Rob have been trying for a baby for many years now. It's not something we talk about, and I hate to pry, but it saddens me, as they'd be awesome parents.

"I've got another crazy baby name for you." Myf laughs as I put her down. "Nevaeh. It's heaven spelt backward. I did my usual 'Well, you don't have to decide today, you have a few weeks to fill in the paperwork'."

Myf loves telling me some of the weird and wonderful names she comes across with the babies she's helped bring into this world.

"Want me to fillet, or do you want to cook it whole?" I ask as I slide the fish out of the cooler.

We've congregated in the kitchen where I sit on a stool at the island bench. If we aren't here, then we'll be out by the barbecue. My sister's place is as eclectic as she is, having been built as a tiny worker's cottage and then added to over the decades.

Large folding doors go from the kitchen to the deck, and it seems as if we're half outside already. It's the sort of house I'd love to live in, one where the kitchen is the centre of everything and where people gather.

"I've got some herbs in the garden we could stuff it with and some limes." Myf has it all under control.

My sister's propensity to talk is perfect for me, as I love to sit and listen. She prattles on about work and some show she's been binging on telly. I won't need to watch it now, as she's given me a blow-by-blow of every episode so far. Sometimes, I think she could write scripts for funnier shows, but she's happy bringing babies earth-side as she terms it.

"And Rob's getting closer and closer to finishing his book, aren't you, babe?" She kisses her husband on the cheek as he slides behind her and reaches for some tongs.

Rob's been writing this book since I've known him. He won't let me read or critique it, and I have to wonder if Myf is biased when she keeps raving about how good it is. I know he loves being a legal secretary, but I wonder if there's more that he's destined for. I've suggested he study law himself, but he simply laughs at the idea. Maybe he is writing the next great Australian novel.

"And did you catch her after work yesterday, mate?" Rob asks me as he snaps the tongs in my face. "Organise a hot date?"

I rub my hands up and down my face, dislodging my glasses.

"Who, the lawyer woman? I thought that was what last weekend was for." Myf slides her arm around her husband's waist, the two of them ganging up on me.

"Look"—I sigh—"it's not a good idea to start workplace relationships, okay?" I know I don't sound convinced.

Rob makes chicken sounds that are incredibly realistic and reminds me of the ones that live at the bottom of their yard.

"I'm not a teenager, alright? I should never have mentioned that I like Val to you." I point at Rob, but there's no venom in my words.

"Perhaps you should have had that as one of your truths and lies. You know, 'I've got a massive crush on a colleague'." Rob's shoulders shake with amusement.

"Yeah, well, you told everyone you were married to my sister with yours." I chuckle to myself that Rob thought he could convince any of our colleagues he had been a professional ballerina.

Rob turns the conversation back to Val. "Even if you hadn't said anything, I think I would have picked up on the way your eyes follow her or the puppy dog looks you send her way."

"Is she gorgeous?" Myf asks.

"She's not ugly, but probably not... I don't know. Perhaps Rhys can tell us more." Rob scrunches his nose. I know he only has eyes for my sister, and I wonder how he can describe Val as simply 'not ugly'.

"She's gorgeous," I reply. "She's got short sort of blonde-browny hair, and a button nose, and these rich eyes that are framed by the longest lashes. And she's funny and witty, and... Yeah, okay, I'm attracted to her." I drop my head on the bench in front of me and think that, yes, I am acting like a lovesick teenager.

"Well, Janet was asking me earlier in the week if you're single." Rob wiggles his eyebrows suggestively.

"Wait, who's Janet?" Myf asks as she slaps her hand on the bench. "Is she another option for my brother?"

"Nah. She's with Penny, and I think she's about to propose to her girlfriend. But she is Val's friend." I tell her as Rob continues to grin. I feel like he's holding something back, but to be honest, I think I'd rather not know.

I don't want to be the laughingstock of the firm. I worked at a larger firm straight out of uni where there was always office drama happening. Hutton Law seems different. Sure, we're a smaller practice than most, but Katherine and Max trust us all. They've said I can work from home as much as I like. They don't micromanage billable hours, and there's never any talk at staff meetings of people not pulling their weight. Max described it to me as swings and roundabouts. He seems to think that things even out over the year, and I tend to believe him.

It would be awful to start something with a colleague, only to have it fizzle out and then have to see them at work. I know I can spend days on end out of the office, so I'm not totally worried about it, but I am wary of my heart being hurt in the process.

"How was your weekend?" Janet asks as we stand in the kitchen at work eating the most delectable cake I've ever tasted. I can taste pineapple, but it looks like banana cake with cream cheese frosting.

"Yeah, good. Had dinner with my sister and Rob on Saturday night. We rang Mum and Dad together." I chuckle, thinking back to the call.

Myf and I worked out when she started uni that if we spoke to them together, we could direct and divert the conversation in a way that suited us. When I told Janet last week about my upbringing and the way Myf and I gang up together when it comes to our parents, she thought it was hilarious.

"I still can't believe you were raised by hippies." Janet shakes her head, a wide smile on her face. "Oh, and I think Val was looking for you before." Janet could be a poker player with the lack of expression on her face. Her tone shows a smirk, but her face is totally neutral. She gives me a wave as she leaves the room.

My heart is racing, knowing that the woman I can't stop thinking about is looking for me. She walks into the break room and catches me licking frosting from my finger and smiles as she pours herself a coffee from the pot on the bench.

"Morning. It's nice to see you in the office. Don't you usually work from home?" Val asks as she stirs some milk into her brew.

"Yep. It was one of my stipulations when I moved here. I often meet clients at home, too, but today, I had to see someone in an office, and I need to check Rob's actually here and working."

"Rob would have to be one of the hardest working secs in there." Val laughs, and I think I could listen to that sound all day. "I mean, he keeps all the women on their toes. It might have been nice if we had had a Christmas party, and we could have seen who he would have brought with him as a partner."

"Well, he would have brought my sister, as the two of them have been together for years." I smile. "But you know that now after his truths and lies."

I cross my legs as I lean against the counter, trying to look cool. I want to appear calm and composed, but inside, I'm fighting a war to not simply demand we have dinner together this week and also reminding my cock that just because I think about her when I stroke it, it doesn't mean it's playtime now that she's here.

"That's nice. My brothers have all been married and partnered up for ages, too."

"All doctors married to doctors?" I ask with a smile as I grab a cup and decide to pour a coffee. The reality is I need something to do with my hands.

"Are you still on about lies and truths?" There was that laugh again. I hadn't seen Val to confirm which were truths and lies yet, and I wasn't sure if she knew which was my furphy.

"Maybe." I smile as I stir milk into my coffee. I usually drink it black, but the milk is next to her, and it gives me an excuse to lean in closer. "You should try that cake. It's divine, like honestly, the best thing I've ever put in my mouth."

*Smooth, Evans. Fuck. I'm blowing this.*

"Really?" Val shoots her head back as if she doesn't believe my words, but she doesn't take a slice. "Actually, can we grab an office to have a chat?"

"Sure." I am most intrigued. Rinsing off my spoon, I place it in the dishwasher before following Val down the corridor. I try not to walk too close to her. Part of me is excited knowing we'll be talking, the other part of me is petrified I'll make a fool of myself.

We find a meeting room at the end of the hallway where we know we won't be disturbed. We take a seat on either side of the round table. People are always barging in and out of our offices at work, and it's unusual to have the door closed, unless we're on private calls. If Val and I were caught alone in her office, or even mine, it would be around the building before someone could say office romance.

"So, tell me about this condo of yours." I try and sound calm, but this is the first time Val and I have been in a room by myself, and my heart is racing.

"I live in a cottage," Val says, her hand waving in the air and her eyes rolling.

"No way. Wow." I shouldn't be surprised. I can see Val pottering around a house like Myf and Rob's. If I think about it, she doesn't strike me as the sort of person to live in a modern condo. Leaning back, I cross my legs. I want to tell Val how gorgeous she looks in that grey pants suit. She'd be almost corporate, except for her hot-pink belt. I love that she's wearing flat shoes as well.

"Yeah. So, my parents are hugely into Valentine's. It is their wedding anniversary—their fortieth this year—and Dad turns sixty-five on the thirteenth, and Mum turns sixty-three on the fifteenth. And me, being the stubborn, strong-willed woman—I like to at least pretend—I am, refused to be born on my due date and came a week late, so I turn thirty on the twenty-first. I think my birth was meant to be their tenth anniversary present or something, but I still wonder if I was planned or an oops." Val's brows crease as she talks about her family. Her words indicate love, but she appears conflicted.

"Hence, you got Val for Valentine?" I ask with a chuckle.

"Don't laugh. It means strong or brave. It doesn't even mean love. Mum wanted Valentina to begin with. If I was a boy, I would actually have been called Rhys because, apparently, that does mean love."

"Interesting. I was always told it meant enthusiasm or passion. So, you're the baby girl after three boys?" I take a sip of my coffee, glad I added the milk, making it a temperature I can drink straight away.

"Yeah, and I turned out to be a tomboy—so much for that." Val laughs.

I glance at my watch. "I have a meeting in five minutes. What can I help you with?" I need to know why we're here.

"Okay… so, this is Janet's idea and not mine, and it doesn't mean anything, so please don't read into it or anything. I grew up in Cassowary Point, and every five years, Mum and Dad organise a huge Valentine's gala night where they raise money for the cardiac department at the hospital where they both work. Mum and Dad, well, especially Mum, keep harping on about me still being single, and she and my youngest older brother and his wife, who was my best friend growing up, are always trying to find a doctor to marry me off to. And I don't want to marry a doctor, and the ball's coming up—"

"Okay, I'll do it." Fuck, I hope I've read this right. She's gearing up to ask me to be her fake boyfriend, isn't she? Shit, I've read enough of those books to see the signs. Except in those books, the couples usually end up together.

"But I haven't asked you."

"You want me to be the pretend boyfriend for the weekend?"

"Well, I mean, I was thinking you wouldn't have to attend, and we could FaceTime them and pretend we were together or something. I mean, you've probably got a girlfriend or something, anyway." Val shakes her hand in front of her. I can't tell if she wants me to have a girlfriend or not.

"Nope, I don't, but it sounds like it could be fun. I love Cassowary Point. Count me in." This could be fun, or it could be a disaster.

"Dad is still fairly traditional, so I can arrange separate rooms and all that, no doubt. Are you sure you're up for this?" Val sounds concerned.

I'm not sure if it's the prospect of spending time with me or the idea of fooling her parents.

"Why not? But I have a few stipulations." If this doesn't work out, I need not only an exit strategy but a way of protecting my heart.

"Okay..." Val bites her bottom lip.

"We need to get some stories straight beforehand so we aren't caught out, so we will need to spend some time together prepping." This I'm more than fine with.

"That sounds fair enough." Val nods her head.

"We keep this quiet. No social media, no rumours around the office." The last thing I want is speculation and a hostile environment for either of us.

"Perfect by me, I don't date colleagues. And, I mean, come the sixteenth of February or whenever you fly home, it will be all over anyway, and we go back to being colleagues." Val's eyes are wide. I wonder if she's surprised I've agreed to this.

"Thank you. That was my third stipulation—an end date. Looks like you have yourself a fake boyfriend."

We shake hands, and it's done. I have six weeks to convince Valerie Hartman that I'm more than the perfect fake boyfriend. I'm the perfect man for her.

# 5

# Val

I thought Rhys Evans was going to laugh at me. I thought he'd say no. Never in a million years did I think his answer would be a yes, or that it would have stipulations. His terms make sense. I don't want people around here thinking we're together when it's only pretend, and I don't want it spread over social media. Fortunately, I'm always forgetting to post the photos I snap anyway.

"You look happy with yourself." Janet pokes her head inside my office. I should be working, but instead, I'm reliving my conversation with Rhys.

He appears to be such a lovely man. I know when he's in the office, he'll always take time to sit in the break room for lunch, and others seem to know plenty about him based on him not winning the truth and lie competition at the retreat. He's also hot. I think it's his square jaw that just makes him look so manly.

The last guy I went out with was a tradie—an electrician. Sure, there's a time for those cargo pants tradies seem to love and high-vis shirts, but seeing Rhys in well-tailored trousers, a crisp white shirt, and a striped tie that included thin stripes of blue that brought out the blue in his eyes was pretty sexy.

"Shut the door," I command with a loud whisper and usher Janet to a seat. "Rhys has agreed to be my pretend boyfriend for the gala, but no one at the office is to know, okay?"

"Excellent," she exclaims. "That should at least get your mum off your back." Janet shimmies in her chair, a huge grin on her face. "He really is a beautiful soul. You may find you get to know him, and next thing, you're living your own happily ever after."

"I doubt it." I shake my head, "We've got an end date anyway if I don't scare him away first with, well, me being me. Plus, I don't do office romances."

"Don't be so hard on yourself, Valerie Hartman," Janet scolds. "You're such a wonderful person yourself, and I know Rhys will see that soon, if he doesn't already."

Maybe he will, but he'll also see how scatterbrained I can be. I hope the arrangement will appease my mother at least, and maybe even my brothers. I think Boyd and Emily want to match me up to a doctor who wants to stay in Cassowary Point so I can move home and be with my family.

Staying in Brisbane has never been the plan.

I wasn't like Emily and in a rush to settle down, though. I wanted to live a little. As soon as I discovered boys, I discovered how much I love sex, or more precisely, how much I love orgasms. I think almost all my friends know that if a guy doesn't give me an orgasm, he doesn't get a second chance.

Being a tomboy growing up, I wondered if I might be more attracted to women. I slept with a woman once, but it did little for me. As Janet pointed out, I need a real-life cock, not a plastic imitation.

I know I could get sex in Cassowary Point, but it's so much smaller than here, and there's less chance of anonymity. Plus, I love my job.

Rhys and I didn't mention sex. It will just cloud things if we go there, so it's definitely best we don't, but it will be a long five weeks being in a man's company and getting to know him with no action.

Needing to plant seeds to make this deception work, I decide I will bypass Mum and go straight to Emily. After all, she's my oldest and dearest friend.

"Hey, Mummy of the Year. How are you? I can't hear Issy in the background. Is she sleeping?" I ask when Emily answers the phone.

"Yeah, she is, and typically, Boyd's at work, so we can't make the most of it." She sounds more despondent than usual.

"Well, hopefully tonight then."

"Yeah, maybe." Her tone is flat, and I can imagine her slumped in one of their comfy lounge chairs.

"You don't sound too hopeful, Em. Is everything okay?" I ask, forcing myself to concentrate and not pick up a file for a client I'm seeing this afternoon.

"You haven't rung to hear of my woes. Tell me some good news, please." I'm almost certain I hear tears in her voice, but I can't be certain. Perhaps I should have FaceTimed.

"Well, I don't know if Mum told you, but I've been seeing this guy from work, and he's agreed to come up for the gala with me." I try to sound excited, but I'm concerned for my friend.

"Oh wow, that's awesome news. He must be pretty special." Emily perks up a little, but I still hear the flatness in her voice. She's been wanting me married for years.

"Yeah, he is. His name is Rhys Evans, and he's a partner in the firm here, and his specialty is maritime law. He lives on a yacht, and he's pretty bloody easy on the eye." The more I think about Rhys, the more I realise what a catch he really is. He is probably perfect for this role, and I hope the two of us will spin it easily to my family.

"You went through that sailing phase as a teenager. Don't tell me, if the boat's a rocking—" It's good to hear her chuckle.

"Shut up." I laugh. "Enough about me, how about you?"

"No, I want to hear all about Rhys."

"Well, he's tall with straight blond hair that is longer on top, not like Boyd though." Boyd has shoulder length hair that he loves to tie into a topknot. "He's got this runner's physique."

"And long fingers?" Emily seems excited all of a sudden.

"His fingers go alright." I try to deflect. I've never really studied his hands, but I'll make a point of it now. "Now, how about you?"

"I think Boyd's having an affair." Emily bursts into tears. "He never wants to touch me, and we haven't had sex since Isobel was born."

I think back to my conversation with Giles. "This is Boyd we're talking about. He's had a crush on you since we were, like, teenagers. He adores you." Boyd and Emily have been together for over fifteen years and married for the last eight. Boyd had always worshipped the ground Emily walked on. "Have you talked to him?"

"I tried, but he's working so much, and he's finishing his training and so close to being a consultant, and a new paediatrician is working with him, and she's just gorgeous, and I know she's single, and she was all over Boyd at the Christmas party." Emily barely takes a breath. "I don't know what to do. But enough of my woes, I want to hear more about your man. He sounds too good to be true!"

"Em—" I start in a soft tone.

"No, Val, please." Emily is trying to stop crying. "I shouldn't have said anything. Please, tell me more about Rhys. I need the distraction. He really sounds perfect for you."

I don't want to distract my best friend, but she doesn't want to talk. It's never been strange having her partnered up with my brother. In fact, it's been wonderful for the most part. When I saw them last, he gave no indication that he wasn't as besotted with her as he always has been.

"Yeah, perhaps he is. I mean, it's early days, and if it wasn't for Valentine's, you probably wouldn't get to meet him until Easter, and it might be all over by then, anyway."

"Why? Are you doubting yourself already? Don't, Val. You're an amazing woman and would be the perfect catch."

"Well, maybe I don't want to be caught. I don't know." I play with a pen on my desk, tapping it from side to side against the file I need to read.

"He must be special if we are all meeting him. Hills will have you engaged by the end of the gala." Emily has stopped sobbing, but I can still hear her sniffles.

I have no doubt my mother will try something like that, but I also think Rhys and I are smart enough to figure out ways of diffusing things. Right now, though, I'm incredibly concerned about Emily and Boyd's relationship. I want to talk more about it, but Issy wakes up, and Emily signs off.

It reminds me that I am so far from them. I loved it when they lived down here for a bit. Emily and I would go to the movies when Boyd was working and she had time off. There's a pull to go home to where I grew up, but there's still something stopping me.

I hate to think something is wrong with my best friend's marriage. I can't imagine Boyd being unfaithful, but then again, stranger things have happened, and I've helped individuals extract themselves from what they thought had been a perfect marriage.

> If I find you have been screwing around on my best friend, I will not only cut off your cock with a rusty knife, but I will make sure she has the best legal advice she can get, and she will hang you out to dry. Remember, I do this for a living, and if it comes to it, she is closer to me than my brothers, so watch it.

Although I feel a sense of satisfaction texting my brother, I wonder if I've gone too far. In less than a minute, my phone rings.

"Val, it's Boyd," I hear between sobs. "How could you think... I've been unfaithful to... the... most perfect... woman in the world?"

"Come on, dickhead, deep breaths." I rub my hand over my forehead.

"I'm sorry. I just can't do anything right." Boyd is still sobbing.

"What do you mean?" I ask, almost dreading the stupid things I know are about to spew from his mouth. I mean, this is my brother we're talking about.

"For ages, I'd hold her and just snuggle, but then she told me I was suffocating her. Then I tried to do more around the house, and it never seems to be enough." Boyd sounds exhausted.

"You're not going to get a fucking medal for doing stuff around the house, idiot. The idea of men's work and unpaid women's labour is long gone. So, you aren't screwing the new paediatrician at work?" A notification pops up on my computer screen, alerting me to my client's arrival. They'll just have to wait a few minutes.

"Who? Melody? Fuck no! Never stick your dick in crazy." His voice is higher than normal.

"Well, Emily seems to think—"

"I could never cheat on Emily. She's my only, always, and forever. I adore her to bits." He starts crying again. Deep down, I knew I should not have doubted my brother.

"Well, she's gagging for it, and she thinks you must be getting it elsewhere," I tell him.

"But I'm scared I'm going to break her," he almost whispers.

Emily had a traumatic labour and birth. They had to cut her to make room for forceps and basically dragged Isobel out. I can only imagine the pain and the trauma healing afterward.

"For fuck's sake. I'm not a doctor, and I know that many people manage to have sex after a baby is born. How would you explain Henry, you, or me otherwise? Talk to Giles or something. I'm sure he can help. Or even Bridget. I mean, she's the obstetrician in the family." I'm so not used to my family approaching me for medical advice.

"You think so?" He sounds so lost.

"Nah," I reply. "Sex is overrated, and you never need to have it again now you've got a kid. Plus, you've got one on ice, so you might even get another baby without ever needing to fuck your wife again. Lucky you."

"Your sarcasm game is strong, Valerie Hillary Charlotte Hartman." He sighs. "I might speak to Giles though. I mean, it won't be the same, because, clearly, my cock is that much bigger than his, and—"

"Oh, shut up." I can't help but laugh at my brother. "I doubt it's the size of a baby's head, so I think Emily's safe."

"You'd be surprised." I'm glad I have my jovial brother back. "Thanks, stinky. Can you tell her how much I love her when you speak to her again?"

"Tell her yourself. Bloody hell, and I've got a client here. That's fifteen billable minutes I should invoice you for."

"Yeah, yeah." He chuckles. "And, Val, thanks. I'll talk to Giles."

A COUPLE OF DAYS LATER, there are flowers on my desk with a card from Issy saying 'Thank you for helping Mummy and Daddy. Mummy really appreciates it!'

"Knock, knock." Rhys is leaning in my doorway with his arms crossed across his chest. "Nice flowers." He pushes his glasses up his nose. "Are we still on for this project, or has a real-life replacement been found?"

"They're lovely, aren't they? They're from my niece, well, her parents really, as I doubt a six-month-old can order such gorgeous blooms." It's nice seeing him again, especially knowing he's sought me out. "You're back in the office again; people will talk. Are you still okay with the plan?" Maybe he has thought about this and realised how stupid my harebrained scheme is. My pulse quickens both with his presence and his calmness. I've always thought him to be shy, but I suspect he just takes time warming up to people, and I'm kind of glad he's warming up to me.

"No." Rhys smiles. "I mean, yes, all good with it all, although I was thinking we should perhaps start this weekend. How does dinner on Friday sound? Nothing flashy, just a bite to eat." His shoulder slips from the doorframe, and he covers it by taking a few steps and sitting at the chair opposite my desk. From the hallway, I hear a snigger and notice a redness on Rhys' neck. I decide not to ask, assuming it's Rob.

"Sounds good. Sounds great, actually. I'm happy to cook if you want to come to mine. It might be easier to take notes and that, and we won't be disturbed."

"Are you sure?" Rhys clasps his hands in his lap. He looks uncomfortable, and I have no idea why.

He's a highly successful lawyer and really is gorgeous. If I bumped into him in a bar, I wouldn't be apologising, and I'd be making sure we spent the night together. He vacillates from oozing sex appeal to appearing nervous. I'll have to try to get to the bottom of that before he meets my mother, or she'll eat him for breakfast, and the jig will be up.

I give Rhys my address and suggest he calls around after six. Technically, the office closes at midday on Friday, but most of us work until at least four. I know that I would have time to get home, changed, and whip something up. I've got two days to work out a dish.

I was meant to be in court today, but my clients have finally come to an arrangement, and the father is agreeing to sign the passport forms for his two children. Pity he wouldn't do this last October when they had the chance to go overseas for Christmas, but at least they will be able to plan something for the future. I'll now have time to work out what I'm going to cook and might even spend some time browsing for new recipes.

I'm flicking through the usual sites I browse for inspiration and come across a curry recipe. It reminds me that I have an almost brother-in-law who makes the best Sri Lankan curries I've ever tasted.

> Can you please send me a recipe for a curry that's not too hot and okay for someone who might not like curries?

KEN

> Um...

> Shit. Maybe I should ask what he likes to eat.

KEN

> Is this your new man?

> No secrets in this family. I'm cooking for him Friday night.

KEN

> If you think he might balk at the idea of a curry, why not pasta? Henry cooked me spaghetti carbonara the first time he cooked, and it's still ingrained in my memory. Actually, might get him to cook it tonight. It has this awesome mouthfeel and slides down your throat.

> Stop sounding so sexual.

KEN

> *smiley face emoji*

> Thanks.

KEN

> All good. Hen and I need to talk to you at some stage. Maybe chat this weekend?

> Yeah. I mean, not Friday night, obviously.

KEN

If you're busy all weekend...

Shut up!

KEN

His orgasm game must be strong.

I love Ken. I'd almost fucked over their relationship when it was in its early stages by offering some pretty poor advice. But I was young, and I didn't really know any better, but it showed me how important communication is in any relationship.

It's probably good that Rhys and I have these ground rules. Sure, I've told Janet, and no doubt, Rhys has told Rob. No one else at the office will ever find out, though. We've got an end date set. I mean, I'm flying back to Brisbane Monday evening after the gala, and I don't think Rhys has booked flights yet. I should make a note to find out when he wants to fly, and I should book them, because he's doing me a favour.

Part of me thinks this is the stupidest decision I've ever made. Fortunately, Rhys seems like such a nice man that I know it won't be hard to act like I'm really into him. Perhaps the worst part will be keeping my hormones in check and not reacting to his sexiness, which I'm noticing more and more.

I slip my chair back from under my desk and blow out a long breath. I need a break from this space. It's almost lunchtime, and I didn't bring anything, thinking I'd grab something at a café near the courthouse. There's a deli down the street, and it's not like I don't have time for lunch today.

I tap on Janet's door, which is open, and think back to how Rhys casually leant against mine this morning.

"Aren't you meant to be in court?" There's a look of fear on Janet's face as she checks her watch and realises what the time is.

"They came to a resolution last night. Lunch? I was going to head to the deli."

"Let me think about that. I mean, a plastic cheese sandwich that I was going to toast and have with a cup of soup or a fresh salad from Marcellas where I can pick up some of the olives Penny adores." Janet grins as she grabs her purse and phone from her drawer before we head out.

It's a warm day outside, but there's a pleasant breeze that brings the scent of the sea, which we are near. Our firm takes up three storefronts on the main street. Some of our offices are upstairs, mine included, with meeting rooms on the ground floor with larger offices for the partners. It's an older building set in a strip of shops on the main street of a beachside suburb. My cottage is about a fifteen-minute drive away, and I'm fortunate that I'm usually travelling against the traffic to and from work.

"I see Rhys is in the office again today." Janet wiggles her eyebrows at me from over her sunglasses.

"He is, and he popped into my office." I try to sound measured and unaffected by the visit, but his nerves still have me concerned we won't be able to pull this off.

"Really?" Janet grins and balls her hands into fists as she shakes her hips from side to side. Her enthusiasm makes me laugh.

"Yeah. We're having dinner Friday night."

"Ooh, like a date?" Janet grabs my arm as we enter the deli, and I slide my sunglasses on top of my head.

"No, like a reconnaissance mission, where we're going to get to know each other better so we can pull this thing off." I sigh. "It's not a date. It's not what this is about."

Janet ignores me as she places her order. I know the whole fake boyfriend thing was her idea, but really, I don't need the pressure of her assuming we will turn into some fairy tale. She knows I don't date people I work with, and I definitely don't sleep with them. I love my job too much to jeopardise it by creating discord in the office and forcing people to choose sides when things sour, which they inevitably do.

There's a garden area at the back of the deli where we sit and eat our lunch. Janet is complaining about a client who wants things in his contract that aren't, let's say, standard. It's not that they're illegal, but highly unusual, and Janet knows the other party won't sign it with these clauses in there.

I hated contract law at uni, which is strange, as marriage is pretty much a contract. I spend more time ripping these contracts apart, though.

Thinking back to marriages breaking down reminds me of Boyd and Emily. If the flowers hadn't arrived from Emily this morning, I would have booked a flight home this weekend to ensure my best friend was alright.

I've grown up in a perfect family, expecting happy relationships. I know Mum didn't have the same childhood we did, but Dad's parents were around until I was ten, and they were a devoted couple, too. Grandad died of a broken heart ten days after his wife. He really couldn't stand living without her. My parents are the same. Sure, they argue at times, but they're devoted to each other. My brothers have all found partners who complement them, and they all seem to be living their best lives. Even when Emily tried to break up with Boyd when they were going through IVF, I never doubted they'd find their way back to each other.

It's me who's alone. Cut off from them. I'm the black sheep who probably won't settle down. I'll be the cool aunt. The one who spoils them rotten and leaves them all the money I make as a lawyer. I'm not in this for the money, though. I loved working for Legal Aid after I graduated, and I'd happily go back and work for a not-for-profit organisation again.

Marriage won't make me happy. I'm not unhappy, of course, but perhaps unfulfilled. Sure, I have my hobbies. I love to read and cook. Yoga was fun on Monday evening, and I'm planning on going again next week, but it's hardly something that will give me fulfilment. I don't know what I need or if I really do need anything to be different. Perhaps I can be a role model to my nieces that shows that a woman can have a fulfilling life without being a wife and mother. Perhaps that will do.

# 6

# Rhys

Rob's right. I've turned into a soft cock. There's no doubt Val heard him giggle in the hallway like a teenager when my shoulder slipped from the doorframe when I was trying to look oh-so-casual. I'm fucking thirty-four years old, not fourteen.

It hasn't been a hardship spending more time in the office than usual. I mean, I genuinely like the people I work with. I can talk with any of the other women there with no issues, but Val is another story altogether.

Have I ever felt like this about a woman? Probably not. I mean, I've never wanted for female company when I've felt like it. It's not like I've lived life as a monk. But there's something different about Val. I'm not sure I've ever believed in soulmates or finding 'the one', but I want to explore things with her. More than her body, of course, even though I often think about that. She's got curves, that's for sure. The swell of her hips in the tailored pants she wears, let alone the pencil skirt she was in the other day, is femininity personified. I often feel my energy drain from being around people, but this doesn't seem to happen when I'm around Val. It's like I gain energy in her presence. I want to listen to her laugh and talk with her about her philosophies on life. Her family sounds amazing, and I want to learn more about them too.

I'm glad I didn't have to go to the office today. I was meeting a client in a coffee shop at the marina. He's got himself into a spot of bother after mistakenly doing the wrong thing returning to Australian waters. I can't imagine sailing the Pacific with children, but I can imagine a father getting fed up with their moaning and mooring on an island in Australian waters without doing the necessary immigration checks. He'll get a fine, but I'm hoping to avoid any record of the event to make it easier to go sailing again, even if he claims it will be just him and his wife next time.

This is the sort of work I'm often called upon to do. That and setting up timeshares for yachts and assisting with selling craft from small sailing yachts like *Serenity*, to larger vessels owned by the rich and famous. I tend to avoid the larger vessels, though, and they usually prefer to go through one of the larger firms that specialise solely in maritime law. I'm just happy doing my bit in my corner.

After my meeting, I returned to the yacht and got out my shaving kit. I can go a few days without the stubble on my face annoying me, especially when I'm not around the office, but I want to be clean-shaven for Val tonight. There needs to be no reason for her to think that she can fire me from this gig. I'm going to be the best pretend boyfriend in the history of pretend boyfriends.

My anxiety increases throughout the afternoon. I want to buy her flowers, but would that be too much? Then I can't choose between red or white wine, and I'm standing in the bottle shop when my phone vibrates in my pocket.

ROB

Set for tonight? Bought condoms?

Shut up. It's not like that. Do you think I should take red or white?

ROB

Ribbed for her pleasure.

I'm talking wine, you idiot.

MYF

Champagne.

Really?

ROB

No. Val seems straightforward. Don't
overthink it. Grab a bottle of white. Ask
someone in the shop for advice.

Perhaps they have a point. I usually like our group chat, but today it
seems like they're both ganging up on me.

"Um, excuse me." I find an older man stocking spirits on the shelf.
"I'm going to my girlfriend's place for dinner tonight for the first time,
and I want to take some wine."

He looks me up and down as if I've got multiple heads, and I
wonder if perhaps I've wandered next door to the tobacconist.

"Sounds like you're a sure thing. We've got that one at the front on
special, and chicks seem to dig it." He shrugs his shoulders and goes
back to stacking the rum.

I head to the fridge. If 'chicks' dig a wine that's on special, that's
fine, but Val isn't some chick. I want something nice to take along. I
settle on a Chenin Blanc from Western Australia, but only because it's
got a nice label with a picture of a turtle on it.

"That's a nice drop," the lady scanning the wine at the checkout
tells me as she reads the back of the label.

"Are you sure? I mean, I asked your colleague." I scrunch up my
nose, eager for her validation.

"He doesn't drink wine. Now if you'd asked him about beer..." She
hands me my receipt. "I think you've made a good choice."

Have I though? I'm strung out thinking about bloody wine vari-
eties. It's not like I know Val at all, really. Maybe that's what it is. Maybe
I'm scared that once we actually talk, I'll discover all the fantasies I've
had about her are lies, and she's just like every other woman I've ever
dated. In my head, I've created this fantasy that Val and I bounce off
each other and can talk for hours, but maybe we will struggle to find
common ground.

I'm not like my parents, and I don't want to be like my uncle. I
want to find someone to spend my life with, someone to share the
little things with. Sure, I'd love it to be forever, but even if it's not, I'd

love to look back and smile because it happened, not cry because I never tried.

Yeah, I shouldn't be thinking about things being over, but that's my history. I've never been the one ending things despite realising the relationships weren't going anywhere. Well, I suppose I set my last girlfriend free, but I'm pretty sure she knew our views on monogamy were different, and she wasn't surprised when we agreed to go our separate ways.

I'd love nothing more than little Rhyses running around. I'd teach them to sail and fish and help them with their homework. It's not that my parents were selfish, but they never helped me with schoolwork, claiming I was already so smart I didn't need any assistance. They never came to parent-teacher conferences at school, and I don't want to think about that night and what sixteen-year-old me saw.

> Should I take flowers?

MYF

> FFS. No. It's not a date. It's a business arrangement, remember?

> Suppose.

MYF

> Sure, I'll be there in ten. Have you filled the tub?

> Sorry?

MYF

> Oops. Think I just texted my labouring woman to harden the fuck up. Gotta run.

ROB

> See ya, babe. If you aren't home when I get there, come and find me waiting for you in bed xx.

> Family discussion, mate. Family discussion.

It's not bad advice from my sister. I need to remember this is just a business transaction. Nothing is going to come from it, and it's never going to go anywhere. Perhaps Val has a sister I can meet or something, someone who doesn't work with me. I can only hope.

I SIT in my car and look in the tiny mirror in the sun visor to check my hair isn't all over the place. It's not. I breathe into my hand and determine there's nothing odd about my breath. There shouldn't be; I brushed my teeth twice and used mouthwash. It's still before six, and I don't want to seem too eager, so I drive around the block again.

Val lives in an older suburb closer to the city than the beach in what appears to be an old worker's cottage. It's nothing like the condo I imagined. Perhaps this means she doesn't have cats, which is good, because I'm allergic.

Eventually, I pull up outside her house again and give myself a pep talk as I walk up the path to her door and ring the bell. Val looks stunning as she answers. She's in shorts and a tank top with bare feet. How can she be so relaxed when I'm a bundle of nerves?

"How was your day?" I ask as Val takes me through to the kitchen and opens the bottle of wine I bought. This is a good start, and I'm able to let out a quick breath.

The home has been opened up at the back into a large open space. Val has the glass doors concertinaed, so we got to sit on the deck in some really comfortable chairs. She brings out some cheese and crackers, which she places on the small table between us.

"So-so. I was in court this morning. The father can't see where his marriage went wrong and seems to think he should have equal custody of a six-year-old and a four-year-old who hate spending time with him because he tells them all the time what a whore their mother is. Meanwhile, the mother is working two jobs to make ends meet because he has hidden his money somewhere, and I doubt she has time for herself, let alone another lover." I don't miss Val's look of delight as she takes the first sip of the wine. A smile grows across her face, and she closes her eyes and almost lets out a moan. My cock hardens immediately.

"I'm so glad there are people like you dealing with that. I'm happy to stick to the sea." My finger wipes at the drips of condensation around the back of the glass.

"Did you get screwed over in your divorce?" Val looks at me intently, and I appreciate her focus is on me. I've been on dates where women stare at their phones and watch other people in the restaurant, but Val's phone doesn't appear to be within reach.

"I've never been married... Ah! Well done. You figured out my lie, and all before we sit down to eat." Two sips of wine, and I'm relaxed already. I was so nervous about tonight, and yet Val is so easy to talk to.

"Your yacht's not called *Serenity*?" She leans forward and cuts some cheese, her eyes wide as if my life is a gigantic secret.

The reason I didn't win the 'two truths and a lie' is because I think I've told most of the office about my parents and their nutty ways.

"Wrong again." I laugh. "I was homeschooled by hippies until I was thirteen. My uncle was a lawyer, and I spent a lot of time with him growing up. He was an enormous influence on me. I mean, I'd read torts at bedtime from a young age, so law school wasn't that challenging for me."

"So, why the sea? I mean, it's a little niche, isn't it?"

Her tank top bears what I suspect is her former university logo on it, and her shorts that finish just above her knees ride up her leg as she sits back and crosses one long limb over the other, looking relaxed.

"And that's why." I chuckle. "Uncle Derick was a criminal lawyer, and I could never do anything like that. I'm not sure how many criminals he might have helped to get off over the years. I mean, he was selective in his clientele, but you and I both know what sorts it takes to do that kind of law. He lived on a yacht for a while though and got me interested in the water."

"Where does he live now?" She uncrosses her legs and tucks them under her after reaching for some more cheese. It's not like she's fidgeting, but it seems it's hard for her to sit still.

"He died three years ago. Heart attack, aged sixty-four." I pause and cut some cheese for myself. "He'd never married and left a large part of his estate to my sister and me. He went to law school with Max and Katherine and was Max's best man or something. When they approached me about the partnership, I said yes. I feel pretty fortunate to be a partner well before I'm forty."

"Cool. So, you're..."

"Thirty-four. Thirty-five in July." I nod.

"And your sister..." Val slides her legs out again and attacks the cheese.

I love that there's no finesse. She places her glass of wine on the table and grabs an extra cracker to pick up the bit that crumbled when she went to cut her slice. She doesn't seem to give a fuck that she's nibbling on food in front of me.

"Myfanwy, but she'll slap you if you call her that—better to stick with Myf. She's a midwife. She's your age, and you remind me a lot of her, except she's married to Rob, who you know."

"No kids then?" Val is relentless with her questions, but I suppose the plan for tonight is to get to know each other better.

"Not yet, but they're trying. Just don't mention it to Rob at work or anything." I wonder how much I should be sharing.

"It took my brother, Boyd, and his wife years of IVF, so I kind of know how trying 'trying' can be." Val seems to always choose her words carefully. I suspect being a lawyer, it is a given, but she speaks with empathy and compassion.

"So, Boyd is next up from you?" I lean back and cross my legs. It's my time to question her.

"That's right. From the top, there's Mum, who is Hillary, but most people call her Hills, Dad, who is Charles, but everyone calls him Charlie. They're both cardiologists. Then there's Giles. He's also a cardiologist married to Bridget, who's a gynaecologist and obstetrician. They have two daughters, Millicent or Millie, who's thirteen, and Amelia or Mia, who's eleven." Val doesn't pause for breath. "Then there's Henry, who has been with Ken for ten years or so, and I suspect they will get married sometime soon. They're both shrinks. Mum and Dad are fine with Henry being gay and in a relationship with Ken, but they never talk children to them, which makes me laugh, because they always make comments to me. Bloody double standards."

"So, then there's Boyd, who married your friend?" I ask.

"Yep. Boyd is a paediatrician—well, he will be in the next few months—and he's married to Emily, who is a lowly GP, and amazing at her job. They have Isobel or Issy, who is six months old, and they have been together since they were teenagers."

"And then there's the most interesting person in the family, Ms Valerie..." I can't help but smile at her. If I wasn't half in love with her before tonight, I will be by the end of it. She's warm and kind and so bubbly.

"I don't think I'm that interesting. So, yeah, I turn thirty in a few weeks." Val suddenly draws in on herself. I want to ask her about it, but I figure that can come later.

"Do you have a middle name?" I ask.

"Yep." She sighs. "Hillary Charlotte. What about you?"

"Nope, no middle name."

"So, your parents..." I can see Val doesn't want to talk about herself anymore. "Actually, come with me while I cook dinner. We can keep talking around the stove. It's carbonara. I hope that's alright. I didn't know what you eat and don't eat."

"Oh, I eat anything really." I shrug as we stand, and Val lifts an eyebrow at me. I want to say that I'd love nothing more than to eat her, but that would be so inappropriate.

I try to focus on her question about my parents. It's hard to describe Maggie and Tom, and I know my family dynamic is so different from Val's. I'm scared my history will turn her away.

"My parents live in northern New South Wales and are totally self-sufficient," I start. "Mum bakes cakes for a lot of the coffee shops around where they live. I suspect she also makes quite a bit from her Hash Brownies, which she bakes for select clientele. Dad's always done odd jobs and gotten a bit of money here and there. I've always chosen not to ask too much, and they have always provided for Myf and me."

"You're like the black sheep, then?" Val pours boiling water from the kettle into the pot and refuses my offer of help to cook.

"Yeah, I suppose so. I suspect most of the free spirit has been beaten out of me by now. What did you call me, refined?" Val smiles at the sly grin on my face.

It's the self-sufficiency that I think has rubbed off most on me. I never had to make friends at school, because I didn't go to a formal school until high school. There was always Myf and me. Sometimes, there'd be other kids who would come, and we'd bake bread together, or we'd head to their place and help them harvest honey or something.

I pour us both another glass of wine as Val plates up dinner. It looks and smells amazing.

"We can eat here or sit on the deck. Which would you prefer?" she asks as she shaves some more Parmesan on top of the pasta.

"I'm easy. I mean, it's lovely outside, and I don't mind eating on my lap." There's no way my body won't react even more if I'm forced to sit side by side here on the stools in her kitchen or at a small table where our knees might touch. I think I need some space before I do something stupid like drag her to her bedroom.

Fuck, who am I kidding? I'd lift her onto the kitchen bench and eat her out before we made it to the bedroom.

We carry our bowls back outside and sit again in the comfy chairs.

"This is so good," I moan as I twirl the pasta onto my fork. "Did you make the pasta?"

"No, but I can. Emily's Nonna taught us all." Val smiles, obviously recalling happy memories.

"Emily's Italian then?" I ask as I try to slow down and not simply shovel the food into my mouth. It really is that good and better than any I've had in any restaurant.

"No. Her Nonna and Nonno came to Australia as newlyweds. Emily was born in China and adopted. She enjoys telling everyone that her mum's Italian and her dad's got Scottish heritage." I have to laugh. "You've never been tempted to settle down then? No biological clock ticking away in the background?"

"God, I'd love kids, but it would have to be with the right woman. I think I've always been incredibly choosy." I need to keep talking to Val to stop being a glutton.

"How many kids?" Val seems to enjoy her dinner as well.

"Honestly? I, um, don't think I've ever been so candid with anyone before..." I sigh and look out at the yard. Being honest with Val is important, even if I know it doesn't sound very, what some might consider, manly. "I'd like at least three, preferably four or five, but, okay, I've never told anyone this." Val stops, her fork halfway to her mouth. "I'd expect their mother to continue in her career if she wanted to. There's no way I could stand being one of those fathers who goes off to make money and only sees his kids on the weekend. I want to be involved and cut back hours at work and stuff. I mean, I don't want to be with a trophy wife who wants me to take care of her as well as a family, but I want to be there to support her, if that makes sense."

"I thought you were going to say you had kids already or something." Val laughs, but I suspect she's also a little relieved. I'm not sure why, and I'm trying not to read into it. "You are still a bit of a hippie then, aren't you?"

"Maybe. What about you?" I play with my pasta, glad Val didn't seem to think I'm emasculated with my confession.

"I love my nieces to bits and often take off time in the holidays so Millie and Mia can come and spend time with me. We go to the museums and galleries and the gardens, and I love showing them the sights in the city, but I will also admit I miss being closer to home. We've always been such a close family, and I seem so far away down here." Val appears wistful as she talks about her family. It is clear to see how close they all are.

"Do you want any of your own?" I ask.

"Yeah, I think I do. I mean, I've seen what Emily's been through trying to get pregnant and then with a really difficult delivery, but, yeah, with the right man, I'd love to have children." Val's brow creases as she nods.

"Plural?"

"Maybe not five, because I am almost thirty and have probably left that too late, but yeah, I'd like a few at least. I mean, making them is the fun part, and I think I'd always be up for that," Val jokes, and it makes me smile.

Keeping my hands off her is going to be hard, almost as hard as my dick is in my shorts. I'm glad we're sitting here and the bowl is covering what could be an embarrassing situation.

We talk about places we've travelled—Val hasn't travelled much but wants to—and we share stories of bad dates we've been on. I discover we have a similar taste in both books and movies, and Val runs to grab some novels for me to read. She didn't even bat an eyelid when I told her I read romance novels from time to time and that some of my best moves come from the ideas of horny authors.

I look at my watch and see it's well after midnight. The evening has flown, and it doesn't feel like we've sat out here for hours just talking.

"This has been one of the most enjoyable non-date, first dates I have ever been on, Val. Thank you," I say as I rinse our bowls and place them in the dishwasher. Val doesn't rearrange them or tell me I'm doing it wrong, like my last girlfriend, seeming happy I'm not in a rush to leave.

Val touches my arm as I close the dishwasher. "No, thank you. It's been nice, hasn't it? I don't think I've laughed so much in ages."

Her touch is brief, but it ignites something inside me. We make our way down the short passage to the front door. I want to lean in and kiss her, but I need to remember this is simply a business arrangement.

"Look, I was planning on taking *Serenity* out on Sunday for a bit. Do you want to join me?" I ask, my heart hammering in my chest.

It might well be that she's just being her nice self and doesn't think we need to spend a lot more time together. I mean, we've really gotten to know each other a lot better tonight already.

"That sounds lovely." Val places her hand on my arm again, and I feel the sensation burning its way to my brain. "It's been years since I've been sailing, well, not since school."

Be still, my beating heart. Just when I thought Val couldn't be any more perfect, I discover she loves being on the water, too. Could she be any more perfect?

"Well, I'll meet you at the marina at, say, ten?" I hope that's not too early.

"Sounds like a plan." Val seems genuinely excited, and I have to remember to breathe. "Do you want me to bring lunch or anything?"

"Dinner tonight was superb, by the way, and you obviously like to cook, so I won't stop you, but I was thinking of grabbing some seafood and having a barbecue on the deck." The inflection at the end of the sentence probably gives my unsureness away, but Val doesn't seem to mind.

"I'll take care of dessert then." She smiles.

I swear she's looking for a kiss, standing by the door looking up at me and blinking, but I recognise that's me projecting. "Sounds perfect. See you then."

I open the door and walk down her path, my heart full. If she wasn't looking, I'd kick my feet together at the side and pump my fists in the air. Spending time with Val is definitely no hardship, that's for sure.

# 7

# Val

I WAIT UNTIL RHYS IS SAFELY IN HIS CAR BEFORE I CLOSE MY front door and lean against it. What the absolute fuck just happened? That was, like, the best evening I've had with a man in years. Fuck, perhaps the best first date ever.

Except it wasn't a date. My bottom lip is between my teeth, and I know I'm staring off into space. I could have stood here for hours or minutes, but it feels like no time has passed. I wanted to kiss Rhys good-night, but I had to hold myself back. It was an arrangement, that's all.

I thought Rhys was so reserved at work. Sure, he's perhaps a little shy, but tonight, he really opened up. He looked at me when I was talking and didn't interrupt. I appreciated he asked probing questions that made me feel he was listening. He didn't want the conversation to be all about him, as interesting as I found his stories.

His life on a boat over the last few years sounds idyllic. He's sailed from the Gold Coast all the way to Cassowary Point and back again. His major regret was not making it further north into the Torres Strait Islands. I almost blurted that I'd go with him and explore, but we have an expiry date. This is pretend, artificial, and an act we are playing to get my family off my back.

Waking up on Saturday, I keep remembering things about the

evening before. I'm so glad that I've asked Rhys to go with me back home, and I know he's perfect for the project. Five years ago, I could argue I was only in my midtwenties when Mum kept quizzing me about boyfriends, but there was something about being almost thirty that made her matchmaking all that more serious.

The conversation about children and thinking about my nieces made me think that perhaps my biological clock is ticking, and I do need to think about things. Working with many sole parents in my job, I can almost see myself being able to raise a child, but the thought of multiple children alone from the start scares me. Rhys seems like such a unicorn, a man who wants to help raise his children.

Craig was my last boyfriend. We went out for a couple of months. I think I liked to pretend he was everything when I knew he wasn't. He acted all alpha when we were out, ordering for me and telling me to focus on him and not look at other men. At first, I found it endearing.

I soon learnt that he didn't want to give me a say anywhere, though, especially in the bedroom. Sure, it was nice to be bossed around a little, but whenever I tried to take control, he got angry. I tried talking to him about it, and he said I was being a moaning bitch. That was enough of a red flag for me to send him running, except he apologised and I gave him a few more weeks until I realised a leopard didn't change its spots.

The final nail in the coffin was when he laughed when I asked him if he'd take time off work if we ever had kids. He told me that's what child-care was for and even said that if I kept on working, I could find a law firm that paid more, and we could get a nanny.

I don't want a nanny. My parents were both doctors when I was a child. Sure, Emily's mum helped a lot, but both of them took time off to come to school concerts and to spend time with us.

It's hard. I want it all, and I know that's not possible. For me, there's no Venn diagram with marriage, kids, and a career with me in the centre. I'm proud of my work, and I'd love to be remembered as a talented lawyer, but I can't see any way to make everything intersect perfectly and keep everyone happy and sane.

I talked to Katherine about it last year. She admitted that she and Max were never really keen on having children and focused on their careers. She says she doesn't regret it, but I think I would. The concept of finding the right man, though, is frightening. Perhaps Rhys is the centre of his own Venn diagram being an amazing husband, lawyer, and father. And yes, we could probably add in lover, because he gave off amazing sexual energy last night. I don't think he realised he was doing it, either. Or maybe I'm just conscious it's already been a few weeks without sex, and I'm imagining things that aren't there.

Early on, I learnt that it's not the size of the wand, but the magic it weaves. Sure, I've been with big dicked guys who've left me totally unsatisfied, and I'll never forget the four-inched guy I was initially disappointed in unwrapping until he showed me what he could do with that tongue and how he could move those hips that had me actually stay the night, something that is unusual for me.

My thoughts turn again to Rhys and what a remarkable man he is. He appears so levelheaded, I'm surprised he hasn't been snatched up by any number of willing ladies. Maybe it's his shyness. I probably shouldn't ask, especially if we're only really work associates. A text from Janet interrupts my thoughts.

JANET

Deal still on? Did he gaze at you with those piercing blue eyes?

It was lovely, actually. We've got a lot in common, so it won't be hard pulling this off.

JANET

Well, maybe it might lead to something...

Yeah, right. I don't date where I work, and besides, we've got an end date set for the sixteenth, anyway.

JANET

What's next then? Waiting until you head north for Valentine's?

We're going sailing tomorrow if the weather holds.

JANET

You've got me jealous now. That sounds perfect. I'll let you go—I'm trying to work through a contract I should have had finished Friday, and my client isn't happy with me.

Boring! Catch you Monday.

Janet knows I hate contract law, and I'm glad to leave her to it. I'm happy dividing assets and making sure kids are well cared for. Occasionally, I'm able to help couples with prenuptial agreements, even though I hate the idea of them, and I have a good sideline in wills and powers of attorney.

I love my work, and I love the firm I work for. I know there are smaller firms in Cassowary Point. Henry and Ken were telling me last year that the husband of a colleague of theirs works at one such firm. I'm struck again by that awful feeling of wanting to move home but not fitting into my family's world by being the single childless one.

Dad would understand. He'd be sympathetic, but I don't think he'd tell Mum or Giles, or even Boyd, to stop. Giles is the worst. He's still so infatuated with Bridget, which is amazing, but he believes it's just as easy for everyone else to have such a relationship. I know it's not, and I know there are plenty of men out there who are nothing like my brothers or Rhys.

As I look in my fridge, I discover that although I thought I had enough butter to bake two cakes—one for work on Monday and one for sailing tomorrow—my butter container is empty. I flick through one of my favourite recipe books but don't find any inspiration. It isn't until I remember Mum's olive oil chocolate cake that I decide it could be a possibility, however, I discover I only have enough oil to bake one cake. My colleagues are going to have to miss out.

Mum taught me my love of baking. Sunday was always food prep day. Mum and Dad shared the cooking of evening meals, but Mum always made sure we had something sweet to pack in our school lunches. I'd stand in the kitchen and help measure flour and sugar, and she'd always let me decorate them, telling me I always did better than she could. I didn't, of course. My sprinkles were always all over the place, and my forked swirls always looked off. The cakes still tasted amazing, though.

I used to bake for my study group in law school. Janet claims it's what attracted so many smart people to our group. Again, I found it helped me relax. Now, I try to spend time each weekend whipping up a creation I can share with my colleagues on Monday.

I don't have any sprinkles or icing sugar, so I leave the cake plain. It will have to do. I don't actually think I've ever baked for a boyfriend before, real or fake. I just hope Rhys appreciates it.

It takes several changes of clothes until I'm happy with what I'm wearing to go sailing. This surprises me, as I usually just throw something on and go with it. In the end, I settle for tan shorts and a white blouse that I know will cover my neck. I'm prone to sunburn with my fair skin. The firm had caps embroidered with our logo last year, and they are extremely comfortable, so I settle for this knowing my mousey brown hair will just be squashed against my head. I slather my arms and face with sunblock, put on my everyday runners, and set off with the cake I baked.

I have to keep reminding myself it's not a date, because it feels like one. Rhys had texted me details of where *Serenity* was moored, and I think I know the area, but I still set off early.

When I arrive, I take in some deep breaths before locking my car and making my way down the jetty I've been directed to.

"You didn't go nautical stripes?" I'm surprised by Rhys's greeting and his jovial tone.

"Was I meant to? I can go home and change..." I point behind me, my eyes wide and my eyebrows raised. Fuck. I didn't ask if there was a dress code.

"Not at all." Rhys's face drops when he thinks he's said the wrong thing. He almost jumps onto the jetty and grabs my elbow. "Good morning, by the way. I, um, it's just that the last couple of women I've taken sailing have worn the navy shorts and striped T-shirt and turned up with flip-flops, or worse, on their feet."

I don't know whether to focus on the women that Rhys has taken on his yacht before me or question if I have dressed inappropriately. I choose not to ask about the women, as I know it's none of my business. It's purely a natural feeling I'm experiencing, and it's not a sign of jealousy for a man who is simply helping me out.

"I thought about a T-shirt, but I wanted to cover my neck a bit as I burn so easily." Rhys is still holding my elbow, almost scared I'm going to run away.

"You look fine. Honestly, you look, well, more than fine, and you're wearing sensible shoes." Rhys looks me up and down, and I feel slightly self-conscious. He jumps back aboard the boat and holds out his hand to help me on. "Welcome aboard *Serenity*. Here's to a peaceful day."

We motor out of the marina and set sail once we reach the open water. It's a perfect day for it. I went on a sailing camp when I was a teenager and enjoyed it so much that I continued with sailing lessons for a bit, and I was surprised even after many years things came back to me, such as rope ties and nautical terminology. Rhys seems impressed that I can help him with the sails and am not afraid to let a sheen of sweat build on my brow working hard to see us skimming across the water.

We find a lovely cove to drop anchor in for lunch. Rhys has marinated squid and prawns and told me he had caught a fish the day before that he also had filleted. After a rocky start with me thinking I was inappropriately dressed, conversation is easy. I tell Rhys about Ken's curry skills, and he agrees that they sound delicious and promises to send me home with some fish to whip into a curry. I must remember to take extra to work for Rhys to have for lunch one day this week. Except people can't know about us, so taking leftovers for him would probably start tongues wagging. I might just have to invite him over for dinner again one night instead.

Rhys positions the barbecue so the smoke blows away from us, but the smells from it make my stomach rumble.

"Now, if there's anything you don't eat, tell me," Rhys says as he transfers the seafood to a platter, which he places on a table along with a watermelon salad he prepared before I arrived.

"No, I eat anything really." I smile. "I've always been adventurous and never been afraid to put something new in my mouth."

I see Rhys swallow and hope I haven't been too suggestive. I forget that my family has always been extremely open about sex and slot innuendos into almost any conversation.

He doesn't answer, and we eat in relative silence, feeling the boat bobbing in the water and the wind and sun hit our faces. When we finish, Rhys packs away the leftovers into containers.

"I didn't ask, but I wondered if you packed your togs, because I could do with a swim," he says as I lie back in the sun.

"I did, actually, because I didn't think you would appreciate me skinny dipping." Once again, Rhys visibly swallows. I thought he was becoming less nervous around me. Perhaps it's his shyness. I hope I'm not blowing things, and he's still going to be okay to come up for the gala with me. If he can't cope with me, then he won't cope with my mother, that's for sure.

Rhys shows me where to change. I own a bikini or two, but I've packed a sensible one-piece to cover more skin.

"Um, Rhys, I think I've covered my front with sunscreen, but could you just do my back, please?" I appear back on deck with a towel slung over my shoulder.

"Most certainly." His voice cracks as I turn my back to him and offer him the bottle of sunscreen. "I see you've gone practical again with your swimmers. I like practicality in a woman."

"I didn't want to give you any ideas, mister." I laugh and turn my head to see his Adam's apple bobbing.

"I am not complaining, and I, um..." I turn my head back, however, I've seen the redness creeping up his neck. Surely he's not that deprived of female company to have this sort of reaction to me? I need to tone things down. I'm being too much, and I'm going to scare him away and leave myself alone at the gala.

I bite my lip and try to stifle a moan when Rhys applies the sunscreen to my back and massages it in with his firm fingers. A shoulder rub has always not only made me relax, but made my nipples harden too. I thank him and place the sunscreen back in my bag.

When Rhys removes his shirt, revealing he keeps very fit, I'm not prepared, and it's my turn to swallow. When he asks if I can cover his back in sunscreen, I quickly retrieve it. It's a pleasure rubbing it in, and I discover he's very ticklish, which I use to my advantage.

"Are you trying to kill me, woman?" He jerks as I tickle along his side.

"Sorry, not sorry, but it is fun teasing you and tickling you." It's not the teasing I'm enjoying, but the feel of his firm muscles contorting beneath my fingers.

"Are you done yet?" he asks as I make another sweep of his back. It's hard to take my hands away.

"Yeah, suppose so." I sigh. "You might need to rip off your shirt in front of my mother, as she's always complaining Dad won't work out."

"I go to the gym a few times a week and go for a run on most days. Now, are you a strong swimmer, or will I need to watch out for you?" Serious Rhys is back.

"You'll definitely have to watch out for me, because I know where you're ticklish," I joke, and with that, I jump into the beautifully clear water.

The water is calm, and Rhys need not have worried about my swimming abilities. We're unable to touch the bottom, yet I'm fit enough to tread water and spend some time floating and relaxing under the sun.

I've been floating for several minutes, lost in my own world, when Rhys flicks water at me, shocking me and causing me to forget where I am.

"I'm sorry, I'm sorry." He laughs as his arms grab my flailing body around my waist and I try to get my bearings.

"Was that payback for all the tickling?" I chuckle, wiping the water from my face that I splashed there myself in my shocked state.

"Yeah, and I was sick of looking at you all peaceful and Zen."

He's so close to me, and I feel like I could reach and tuck a wisp of hair behind his ear, but I don't. It's not that kind of relationship... it's not any kind of relationship.

"You could have tried it, the floating, I mean." My heart is racing, and it's not just from the shock of the splash of water.

"And have both of us float away from the boat? Look how far away you've drifted already." There's no malice in Rhys' voice, merely concern.

I've drifted about twenty-five metres from the boat and am glad Rhys was looking out for me.

"Do we need to get back?" I ask.

"Are you sick of it out here already?" A look of concern crosses his face.

"No, not at all, no." I grab for his arm. "*Serenity* certainly lives up to her name."

"It's light until eightish, and I can sail at night, but I'm not sure if you have to prepare anything for work tomorrow or anything."

We're both treading water. I can feel Rhys' arm around my waist still, and my hand still touches his elbow. It's so intimate. I want to throw my legs around his waist and kiss him. There's something definitely happening between the two of us, and it makes me a little worried if I'm being honest.

This isn't the plan. I need to keep reminding myself of that. It must be that I haven't had sex in quite a few weeks and my body is missing intimacy. There's no doubt I'm reading things into my contact with Rhys that are solely in my head. I'm projecting and wanting to see things that simply aren't there.

"Nope. I make a point of not working on the weekends," I tell him.

"Excellent. I am so glad to hear." He beams. I love it when Rhys smiles, as there are lines that appear around his eyes. He may seem serious a lot of the time, but it's clear he uses his facial muscles a lot.

"I started when I first joined the firm, and Katherine scolded me and showed me smarter ways of working that can also save clients some money."

"Katherine is such a good egg. I'm worried she and Max are going to retire at the same time, and I'll suddenly be a senior partner. It scares me." Rhys' brow furrows again.

"It shouldn't. You're amazing at what you do, and your clients seem to love you."

"What about you? Is your goal to make partner?" Rhys asks.

"One day, maybe. I don't think it's my driving force. I don't like the idea of large firms with lots of partners. It's one reason I enjoy working where I am. Plus, I still find I get so engrossed in work, I forget things about my non-work life. Take last month, for instance. I forgot my car rego was due, so it was late, and I copped a fine." Being deep in conversation, I don't think Rhys had noticed his arm was still around my waist. It feels normal and friendly and, well, nice. "This swimming has me hungry. I baked a chocolate cake..."

"That sounds about perfect right now. Race you back."

I push away from Rhys' shoulders and set off for the yacht, but Rhys is soon next to me. He never tries to pull ahead and makes me laugh when we both touch the stern at the same time. We climb aboard and are both smiling when he passes me a towel to dry off.

With my shirt flung over my shoulders, I grab the cake from the locker we'd stowed it in and cut us both a slice. I'm pleased with how the cake turned out. I had thought twice about baking for a man whose mother baked cakes for a living.

"This is better than my mum's chocolate cake." Rhys moans as he takes a second bite. "Do you think you could share the recipe? I'm sure she'd love it."

"Yeah, not a problem. It's one of Mum's recipes and one she used to bake on regular rotation when we were growing up."

"You want tea or coffee?" Rhys asks as he places a camp kettle on a gas burner.

"Tea would be lovely, thanks." Rhys licks his fingers again, eager to catch any crumbs. "You don't usually call at the office on a Monday, but our colleagues are going to be a little pissed there's no cake in the tearoom tomorrow morning."

"You mean you didn't bake two? I've been there once or twice on a Monday and never realised it was you who baked. That cake last Monday was sublime, like the cream cheese frosting, oh..." Rhys moans again and clutches his hand to his heart as he gazes heavenward. "I feel privileged you baked for me, and I'm going to cut the leftovers into slices and freeze them, and then I can bring one out and nibble on Val when I feel like it." Rhys pauses, his entire face beet red. "Um, oops. I think that came out wrong. Sorry."

"Nibble on me, hey? I'm glad you liked the Hummingbird Cake. It's one of my favourites. I might have to bake that for you too to nibble on some time." I could see Rhys was still a little unsure of how to take me, but my smile was matched by his.

"Changing the subject from cake—as loathe as I am, because cake should be one of the five food groups—when are we expected up north?" Rhys places tea bags in mugs and pours the boiling water on them.

"I've booked to head up Thursday afternoon and come back Monday evening. This was done before our arrangement, and if you need to come later and leave earlier, that's fine." I offer as I grab my phone from my bag.

Rhys puts on his glasses and retrieves his diary from his work bag. Everything for me was fully electronic these days, but it looks like Rhys is old school. I find it endearing.

"I could manage that." He scribbles some notes with a lovely fountain pen. "I have a meeting Friday lunchtime I could do by phone, and I like to keep Mondays clear, anyway."

"If you wanted to fly up Friday, it wouldn't be a problem at all," I offer.

"Are you sure?" Rhys is flicking from one page to another. "It's one of my big clients. I could see if he'll move?"

"No, don't be silly." I lean over and tap his arm. The touch is electrifying. "I'll be able to sing your praises for twenty-four hours, and it will reduce the acting time for both of us."

"How about I move the meeting to the morning, and I catch the lunchtime flight?" He looks at me.

"Perfect. I'll book for you." I smile.

"Don't be silly," he scolds. "I'm looking forward to a weekend away."

"The gala's black tie. Do you own a dinner suit?" I close one eye and bite my lip. I know I'm asking a lot.

"I do. It's not often I get to wear it either, so it will be nice to drag it out." Rhys appears genuinely excited about our weekend away. I'm just glad I haven't scared him off yet.

"Cool. Henry has organised red silk bow ties for the men, and he messaged me last night to say that he has one for you. It made it all seem that bit more real, I suppose. You're still fine with the plan?"

"Of course." Rhys looks surprised I might not be. "You don't have your diary with you, but I was going to suggest lunch one day this week."

"I'm electronic, baby." I wave my phone in the air before swiping to open the calendar app. "Always have my diary with me. Like I said before, if it's not in my diary, I'll forget about it; my forgetfulness is a running joke amongst the family. Let me see, I'm in court Tuesday and Friday. Wednesday or Thursday's looking good. Or even Friday. It shouldn't be a long hearing, and I know it's with Magistrate Wilkinson, who hates working Friday afternoons."

"Lock-in Friday then. I'm looking forward to it." Rhys's smile is infectious.

I'm just surprised that after a weekend of getting to know each other, Rhys hasn't run for the hills. Sometimes, I think I must be a walking, talking red flag. Perhaps Rhys simply hasn't noticed yet. Perhaps he's the type of guy who will commit to something and see it through, even if it pains him.

Whatever it is, I'll make sure he has an enjoyable time during the gala. I'll need to think of something to thank him for all of his help. If only I could offer him my body.

# 8

# Rhys

I'm gone. There's no hope for me. After an evening at her place and a day on *Serenity*, I'm more than half in love with Val already. She keeps asking me if I'm sure about the weekend with her family, like I'm going to pull out or something. I never could. I'm in too deep.

The flashbacks of putting my arm around her in the water and pretending to keep her safe are never far from my mind. We were so close. The zing whenever she put her hand on my arm. Wowsers. I'd usually berate myself for resorting to talking about work, but the conversation was secondary to the physical proximity of the both of us. Just being that close to the woman who I've been dreaming about for months was enough.

As much as Val is outgoing and bubbly, there's an insecurity I can see under the surface. I want to tell her how amazing she is and even what she perceives as imperfections all make up the perfect package that is Valerie Hartman.

It's a stunning evening on deck, and I wish Val had stayed longer. Myf started blowing up my phone with messages, and Val made excuses to leave.

I went through a Keira Knightly phase some years ago and

watched Pride and Prejudice several times. The scene where Darcy helps her into the carriage and then flexes his hand in response to her touch has always stuck with me. Well, I felt every bit of what Darcy suffered at the touch of the woman he loved from afar when I helped Val up onto the dock as she was leaving. She insisted I didn't need to walk her to her car and, of course, my phone beeped again with another message, but my hand lingered, and I couldn't help but notice Val's smile.

Perhaps I'm living my own period drama where there's no kissing and definitely no sex. I know bikinis are sexy, but seeing Val in the one-piece suit was one of the sexiest things I've ever seen. It was navy with pink trim and really highlighted her curves and her sex appeal. Even in my baggy board shorts, I'm sure she could have noticed the tent that pitched.

In my twenties, I was as carefree as I suspect Val is. Despite my shyness, a few drinks, and I'd make sure my bed wasn't empty for the night. Things changed after Derek died, though, and I bought *Serenity*. Some women think it's sexy living on a sailboat. I learnt early on that if I call it a yacht, they think it's one of those superyachts owned by the rich and famous and get almost disappointed when they discover how poky my living conditions really are. Now, I tell people it's like living in a tiny house.

I could tell Val loved being onboard today. She simply fit in. From our conversations, I knew she had some sailing experience, but seeing her know when to step in, and taking instructions like a pro, was really impressive. She didn't want to lie on the deck and sunbathe, like most women I've brought out on her.

It was tempting to kiss her, even leave a peck on her hand as I helped her ashore, but I'm not convinced this is all simply an act for Val. As lawyers, we get used to acting. I've had to stand up in court and defend people by stretching reality. That's what Val and I are doing. We're pretending. I need to remember this, otherwise, I'm going to get hurt—devastated really.

My phone beeps again. I need to see what Myf wants.

MYF

How did you go?

MYF

I mean today, with Val.

MYF

Is she still there?

MYF

I'm going to ring you if you don't answer me.

MYF

Okay, you know I won't, because I hate speaking on the phone.

MYF

Did she throw you overboard?

MYF

Val, if you're there reading this and you've left Rhys in the ocean, he probably deserves it. He told me you've got older brothers, so I guess you understand how revolting they can be. Not that Rhys is that revolting.

MYF

I mean, he's really nice, and you should get to know him.

MYF

I think I might drag Rob down to the marina with me to see how you are.

MYF

...

Fuck off. I'm here, and she's just left because you kept blowing up my phone.

MYF

...

> Don't type an essay, and don't apologise, because I know you're not sorry. Also, don't come down here. Today was lovely. Val's lovely, but this is just a business arrangement. We're creating a story to get her parents off her back. That's all.

MYF

> Whatever you need to tell yourself, bro.

I love my sister, I really do. I know our parents think we've both sold ourselves out to the corporate juggernauts and embraced capitalism, but I don't think we're that bad. My parents might object to the concept of marriage, but they attended Myf and Rob's ceremony, even if they embarrassed some of Rob's friends. I think Myf and I are used to their behaviour now.

Myf cares in her own way. She knows what I saw that night when I was sixteen, and even if I can look back with adult eyes now, I can't say I'm over it, nor will I ever will be. I protected her when she was a teenager, even if it meant telling her about our parents. They thought we knew. Myf may have had an inkling, but I had no idea. Maybe if I'd embraced their hippie lifestyle, I might have cottoned on earlier.

"Hey, Rhys." Klaus waves as he walks down the jetty. He's moored a few berths down from me. "We're cracking open some coldies. Come and join us. Martha's made some goopy thing to have with carrots."

I get on well with both Klaus and Martha. When their youngest went off to uni, they sold the family home and moved onto *Aboat Time*, the yacht they'd spent their weekends building for many years. Klaus still works as an architect, and Martha does some relief teaching a few days a week.

I pocket my phone and lock up. The marina is fairly safe, but I worry all the same. I jump onto the dock and make my way to Klaus and Matha's vessel. Martha has fairy lights lit and is sitting back with a glass of wine in her hand.

"Rhys." Martha jumps up and kisses me on both cheeks, her hands gripping my arms. "Now who was that gorgeous woman on *Serenity* today?"

Klaus twists the top off two beers and passes one to me. We clink the necks together.

"She's a colleague, that's all," I offer as I perch on the seat I usually take.

Both Martha and Klaus are younger than my parents, but they fill a Maggie- and Tom-sized hole. It's not that I don't speak to my folks, but they make it hard, refusing to own a mobile phone and only checking their email once a week if we're lucky. It's Dad's birthday the weekend after next, and I should go down and see them, I think to myself.

"Well, she looked like she knew what she was doing when you got back here. I hope we'll see more of her. Now, have some dip. It's a new recipe." Martha smiles as she pushes the bowl towards me.

"Oh, wow, Martha," I say between mouthfuls. "This is great. What's in it?"

"Goop," says Klaus as he takes a swig of his beer. I love how he likes to rile his wife up.

"Shut your mouth." Martha throws a cracker at her husband, who throws it on the pier where there are seagulls circling, waiting for a feed. "It's whipped feta with cream cheese, honey, and a few other bits and pieces."

Klaus tells me about the house he's designing for friends of theirs who want to downsize. I love how he's incorporating storage ideas that work well on vessels like ours.

We sit and talk until the sun goes down. Martha tries to get more information about Val, but there's nothing to say. I wish there was, but I need to get any idea of a future together out of my head. Martha eventually changes the subject and rabbits on about their sons and how they're both spending their summer holidays working in bars. Sounds about perfect to me.

I eventually bid them farewell and make my way back to *Serenity*. I'll get up early in the morning and go to the gym—maybe even for a run, depending on the weather. I need to do something physical to get Valerie Hartman out of my head.

"WHAT ARE YOU DOING DOWN HERE?" I ask Rob as he walks down the jetty after I'm back from the gym.

I wasn't lying when I told Val I try to keep Mondays clear. Today, I planned to get into another one of the books she lent me when I went for dinner. I finished one on Saturday, which I loved, and I started a second one last night before I fell asleep.

"I told the girls I was doing a coffee run, but I needed to pop in here first." He's smirking, and I know he's just come to ask me about the weekend.

"It's a long way to come to get coffee." I don't bother moving from my seat on the deck, my leg propped against my knee.

"I'm grabbing coffee from the deli near work. I needed to come and see my boss to find out how his weekend was." Rob jumps on board and places the kettle on the burner, turning it on to heat.

"I thought you were grabbing coffee from the deli." I'm trying not to look up from my book.

"Might have a tea first." He grabs the book from my hand and starts reading the blurb. "Brandon Scallion has never known love, not from his parents, and definitely not from a woman, but when Cindy McDermott waltzes into his life, he soon realises it will never be the same. She goes from being the one needing protection to... Fuck, mate, what is this shit?"

"It's a book. You see, they print words inside, and you read them, and they tell a story." I snatch it back from him. "It's actually not that bad. He's ex-military, and she's a flautist who's attracted the attention... Actually, nah. I don't need to defend my reading choices. But I will say that at least this author actually got around to finishing writing one."

I know that dig will hurt. Rob's a perfectionist and can't seem to commit to sending what I think is now draft five hundred and something of his book off to the editor I found for him.

"How was yesterday?" he asks as he pours water into two mugs before placing the tea bags in. He only does it this way because he knows it irks me.

"It was good. I think Val and I will pull the whole thing off." I tuck the book beside me as Rob hands me a mug. He's chosen lemon and ginger tea, not that I would have complained with any that I have in my collection.

"Well, Val's smiling and a bubbly ball of energy around the office today. Melinda even asked her if she got laid, and she said that she no longer kisses and tells, but that she had a lovely weekend."

My heart races at this news. I know it shouldn't, but surely that means there's some hope, at least. I sip at my tea and contemplate pulling out a slice of cake, but I don't want to share with Rob.

"Oh, and everyone's pissed because there's no cake in the kitchen today." Rob laughs, and I can't help feeling special knowing I have three-quarters of her cake in my fridge and freezer.

"How's Melinda going?" I ask, thinking back to what she divulged about her husband at the retreat.

"She hasn't said anything, and I don't really want to ask. It sounds like her hubby needs the same tough love you gave me early on." Rob looks contemplative as he stares into his mug, his shoulders slumped.

"It's Tom's birthday weekend after next," I tell Rob, changing the subject as I focus on a bird that looks like it's circling some fish.

"Myf was saying. She said we'll probably head down on the Sunday, just so we don't have to stay overnight." I think the jury is still out on whether Maggie and Tom like Rob.

"Yeah. I might do the same." I sip my tea.

"You should bring Val." Rob is all matter-of-fact, but I know Myf wants to meet her.

"I don't think so." I chuckle. "She thinks her mother's forthright. Can you imagine introducing her to Maggie?"

"So, if you haven't worked it out, Myf's dying to meet her. Can you bring her to dinner at ours Sunday night?"

I groan. Meeting Myf will be better than meeting Maggie, and I know Val will hold her own, but she doesn't deserve to be put through it. "I'll ask her."

Rob talks about some things from the office, all of which could have waited, and is on his way.

I appreciate being cared for by my sister and brother-in-law. I just wish they'd left me alone today. There's no need for anyone to micro-manage my life. I'm doing okay. Well, at least I tell myself this. Fake it till you make it or something.

I let out a contented sigh, happy that, at last, I'm alone again. It's a gorgeous day, with the sun beating down and a gentle breeze that cools the sweat that gleams on my skin. Val is never far from my thoughts. Whereas Rob's visit was an inconvenience, if Val walked along the jetty this morning, I would have jumped for joy—well, inwardly, at least.

"MORNING, RHYS," Max greets me as he pours a coffee from the pot in the staff room.

I don't need to be in the office today, but Val said she's in court tomorrow, and I want an excuse to see her.

"Hi, Max. How's things?" I stifle a yawn as I stir my black coffee. I'm so tired, I don't even notice I'm doing the meaningless thing. It's not like I've added milk or sugar. I didn't sleep well last night, a certain lawyer filling my head with images of her in a navy swimsuit.

"Good, good. Did we have a partner's meeting today?" Max scrambles for his phone to check his calendar.

"I think that's next Tuesday. I just need to pick up some things and do some research." Max is another one who notices I'm not in the office a lot, it would seem. I suppose that's to be expected, what with him being a senior partner and all.

"Good, good." This is one of Max's stock standard phrases. I think I could probably tell him that the office was on fire, and he'd give me the same two word response.

"My next few weeks are busy, but I need to have you and Katherine out on *Serenity* again sometime." I like Max and Katherine's company. We spent some time between Christmas and New Year on the water when the office was closed.

"Lock it in." Max smiles, his fingers playing with his moustache. "Morning, Val."

"Hi, Max, Rhys." Val grins when she sees me as she breezes into the kitchen area.

She's wearing a straight grey dress that finishes just above her knees and has some bright-pink beads around her neck with matching earrings. Flat black shoes finish the ensemble. My eyes are on Val, and I don't even notice Max leave the room.

"Hi," I almost croak. So much for being cool and suave. "How are you?"

"Yeah, good." Val pours a coffee, and I pass her the milk. "Just had to explain to a client that the counteroffer from her ex is perfectly reasonable and what I explained would be the best-case scenario when we first met. She's grown greedy, and it's hard to reason with people like that. But enough about me."

I could never hear enough about Val.

"You mentioned an eReader, and I was thinking it might be a good idea, as I don't have room for bookshelves like you do." I lean against the counter.

"That's a great idea. My Kindle's in my office if you want to come and have a look." Val rinses her spoon and leaves it on the drying rack.

I want to dry it and put it away, but I also want to follow her down the corridor. The desire to follow her wins out. Val doesn't set out to be sexy. There's no exaggerated swagger in her hips as she walks, but all the same, I could stare at her curves and walk to Cassowary Point and back following her.

Her office is ordered, if not a little cluttered. She grabs the device from her bag and explains the features of it, most of which mean little to me.

The enthusiasm and lilt in her voice are captivating. She told me on Friday night how she worked in a bookshop when she was at uni, and I can see her selling salt to a slug. It's not a bad skill for a lawyer to have, as long as we use it for good, something I'm sure Val is well aware of.

I listen to her calm manner when a call comes in from a client and love the way she reassures them they need to stick to the strategy they've talked about and reiterates that they are safe, and he physically can't hurt her anymore. It's sobering to hear her talk to this client.

"Sorry about that." Val slumps back in her chair as she hangs up the phone. "I think I act as counsellor half the time."

"You're a natural at it." I lean forward in my chair, wanting to be closer to her.

"I don't know." She scrubs her hands up and down her face. It's not that she needs makeup, but she rarely wears any, and I suspect if she did,

JEZABEL NIGHTINGALE

it would be rubbed off fairly quickly. "I think I need to do another course or something. I have a bit of self doubt at times."

It's the first time Val has vocalised her vulnerability. I've seen it during our conversations, but actually hearing her admit to it makes me want to contradict her. I know this won't help, though.

"Can Henry help? I mean, as a psychiatrist, he should have some counselling strategies you can incorporate, if that's what you think you need." I want to fix things for her.

"Maybe. I just..." Val sighs. "I don't like showing my weaknesses to my family. They expected me to study medicine, and I need to be the best lawyer out there in their eyes to prove I made the right choice."

Wow. I want to reach across the desk and drag Val into my lap so I can hold her and rock her while I comfort her. I'm not sure how much of her frustration is about her client and how much is about her family. She described an idyllic childhood last Friday night and a closeness amongst everyone that sounded almost perfect. I'm a fixer, and I want to fix this, but there's no ideal way to do that I can see.

"I don't think you should doubt your skills as a lawyer, Val," I tell her as I try to sound compassionate. She's concerned about the perceptions of others when I don't think she needs to be. But she also doesn't need me telling her this.

Val doesn't reply. She shrugs her shoulders and scrunches her nose. And I think we silently agree to disagree.

"Don't forget to bill them." I smile as I stand. I need to leave before I do or say something stupid.

I want to tell Val she's perfect and the complete package, but I need to remind myself this isn't real. She can at least avoid some of her family's pressure when I'm with her in a few weeks.

"I shouldn't be telling one of the partners this, but I was planning on forgetting. It's her second call this morning, and I billed her for the first. Combined, they probably make fifteen minutes."

She's smiling again at least as I open the door to her office. "You do you, Val."

I'm smiling, too. So worth coming in today, even if it was for a ten-minute coffee break together.

90

# 9

# Val

THE HEARING ON FRIDAY DRAGS. I'M REPRESENTING A father who discovered his wife had been having numerous affairs, and there were question marks over the paternity of their youngest child. It's getting messy. My client is a lovely man who works hard in his cleaning business and can only contest his ex-wife because his parents had come into some money and could help.

She's gone with a large firm and has a lawyer who makes my skin crawl. I know he's still annoyed that I rejected his advances at a law ball some years ago. If his wife wasn't there, I might have agreed to give him a go, but I don't fuck married men. I roll my eyes, noticing he still isn't wearing a wedding ring.

"You were amazing up there." I hadn't realised Rhys had stepped into the back of the courtroom. "I forgot how much fun it is representing someone in court. It's not often I do it these days."

My client has had to rush off to work, and I'm still gathering my folders together. Rhys grabs the largest folder and tucks it under his arm before we move to leave the room. I smile at him as he holds the courtroom door open for me. It's a simple gesture, but it adds to the niceness that is Rhys.

It's not that I'm chasing nice, but having someone willing to help is a nice change. I know it's pretend and Rhys and I aren't really dating, but I can't remember any other boyfriend coming to see me in court.

"I'm just annoyed that what's happened to my client is not an uncommon occurrence, and if his parents didn't have money, then it would be so hard for him to fight it. You know I started in Legal Aid and would have continued there, except I was there under a twelve-month contract, and once I had gained the experience, I was moved on." We reach the lift, and I press the button to call it to our floor. It arrives quickly, and we step inside. "And I hate having to sit across from fucking Milton O'Donau. He's everything that's wrong with our profession." I huff as I press the button for the ground floor, glad that we're alone.

"He enjoyed watching you," Rhys offers as we both lean against the back of the lift.

"He's a creep. He doesn't wear a wedding ring but parades his wife whenever he can. Plus, he's always hitting on colleagues."

"Has he hit on you?" Rhys sounds defensive as the doors open, and we leave the lift.

"He tried, but I don't sleep with colleagues." We walk out the glass sliding doors into the warm air. "Or married men, for that matter."

Rhys is silent as I make my way to my car, opening the boot and placing the files in there. I double-check I've locked my car again and suggest a little bistro around the corner for lunch.

Conversation flows freely and is interspersed with lots of laughter. Rhys is a natural storyteller. At first, I thought he was reserved, but he really is coming out of his shell around me. He tells me about cantankerous clients and coming up against a judge in one small town he worked in, who constantly fell asleep after lunch, and how he knew this judge's clerk who would try to work out which cases he needed to ensure were heard in the morning and which would be more advantageous to be heard before a sleeping lawmaker.

The way Rhys talks, I wonder if the clerk was a former lover. It sounds like she bent over backwards for whatever Rhys wanted for his clients, and he smiles when reminiscing about her. A frown crosses my face as I feel pangs of jealousy at someone he may or may not have seen in the past. The jealousy is not only about Rhys' past though. It's also about the fact that he may have had a relationship with a colleague and lived to tell the tale. Law can still be a bit of a boys' club, and I've worked too hard to ruin my reputation by having a relationship sour. I've seen female colleagues have to rebuild their careers after a tiny misstep, and yet, our male colleagues get away with far worse.

It just seems easier for guys. I wonder how she coped after it ended? Jeez. I've really gone off on a tangent here. I don't even know if Rhys and this woman were in a relationship at all. And I'm not about to ask, either.

I glance at my watch and see we've been here for longer than I planned.

"Ugh." My shoulders slump. "I have to go shopping for a dress for the gala, and I hate trying on clothes."

"I can come with you if you like." Rhys finishes his water, and we stand.

"No, I need to do this alone." I blow out a breath through vibrating lips, making a sound that sees Rhys laugh.

"I think you could wear a burlap sack and still be the most gorgeous woman in the room, Val." Rhys looks serious, and my heart swells in my chest. Any insecurity I might have had about Rhys' dating past is soon forgotten.

"Maybe I'll surprise you on the night and turn up in a sack." Rhys just smiles.

I was honest when I told him I didn't date colleagues. None of my brothers met their partners at work, but they are all doctors. Even if I'd met Rhys at uni, I know nothing would have come of it, because I was nowhere near ready to settle down. Now, though, I'm almost annoyed nothing will come of our arrangement. Rhys is awesome. He's easy to talk to, and we have a lot in common. A relationship, though, is out of the question. The two-month mark would come, and we'd be forced to work together even though we'd broken up, and my relationships all end before the two-month mark.

If I'm honest with myself, most of my relationships could have ended around the two-week mark, but I let them drag out, hoping that they might be different. The two-week mark with Rhys is fast approaching, and I have no reservations yet. This is probably because I know we aren't in a relationship.

There's a scuffle between the two of us when we go to pay the bill. Rhys wins in the end and hands over his card, telling me I can get the next one. I look forward to there being a next one. He really is the perfect pretend boyfriend.

We walk back to where I parked my car this morning and part ways with a kiss on the cheek. It isn't forced and seems the natural thing to do. On my way back to the office to drop off my files, I can still feel it, and I bring my hand up to stroke the area his lips touched. I shouldn't have to remind myself that I can't fall for Rhys Evans, but there's something happening between us, and I don't know if I can stop it—or if I want to.

RED IS the theme for my parents' ruby anniversary. I try on several gowns in the first boutique I visit, but none are perfect. I have Emily on FaceTime, and she's poo-poohed all of them too.

"There's still time for me to get Mum to whip something up for you. You should see my gown—she's included these slits that hide under rolls of fabric on the chest, so I can still feed Issy throughout the night." Issy's down for her afternoon nap, and Emily is sounding much happier than she has in weeks.

"Is there any red fabric left in the shops up there?" I joke. "Surely Rosa has used it all already. Anyway, I'll call you back in the next store."

Emily's mum is an amazing dressmaker, and I consider taking up her offer until I get to the second boutique. It's not a place I've been before, but the gowns are stunning. I love that the shelves are separated by colour, and although I'm tempted to look at the gowns in different shades of blue, I head to a wall of red.

My hand trails over the different fabrics. The textures vary from smooth to coarser feeling that I worry will annoy my skin. I pull a few gowns and glance at them before I either ask to have them taken to the change room or place them back on the shelf.

"Do you mind if I add a couple I think would suit you?" the sales-person asks.

"Go for it. I'm not a shopping fan." I huff out a breath.

I like the look of one gown, but they don't have my size. Another goes back on the rack faster than I pull it off when I check the price. I don't think I'll last all night in a gown covered in crystals, anyway.

In the changing room, I try a few of the gowns I've chosen and call Emily back.

"Look, it's nice." I know Emily is being diplomatic. The bows on the shoulders that looked like a nice accent when the dress hung on the rack stick up and aren't symmetrical. I know it's the style, but it irks me.

"I'm not sold on it." I sigh. "Can you see why I hate shopping?"

"What are those gowns over there?" Emily looks around at the camera on her phone as if she'll be able to see to the side of mine.

"They're ones the salesperson put in here, but I don't think they're in my size."

"Try one and see." I love Emily's optimism, but I'm seriously over shopping already.

I slip into one and tie the straps behind my neck. I'd placed my phone leaning up against my purse on a stool in the room, and Emily hadn't mentioned when it toppled over, and she was forced to look at the light fixture whilst I changed.

"Oh, Val, it's perfect," Emily almost whispers as I hold up the phone for her to look. "Rhys is going to love it."

It is indeed a gorgeous dress: ruby-red silk organza in a halter neck style, fully backless with a flowing skirt with a long slit through which I could still poke a leg if I wanted.

"I think I'll still need a bra with it though, and it doesn't have a back." I turn to show Emily, just as the salesperson enters the area with yet another gown.

"Darling," the salesperson drawls. "That dress was made for you."

I know it's her job, but the way her face lights up when she sees me shows I might be onto a winner.

"She thinks she needs a bra, but tomorrow, she'll be complaining her tits are too small again," Emily tattles down the line. I give her a glare, and she pokes her tongue out at me.

"We've got tape and also these sticky rabbits. Both will ensure those puppies stay in place all night long. Your boyfriend's going to love it. Now, the shop next door sells lingerie, and if you tell them I sent you, they'll fix you up with some stunning knickers that will drive your man wild. I'll get the dress ready for you and see you back here after, alright?"

I nod, almost hesitant to get out of this gown. I never would have thought to go backless before. My mind drifts to Rhys applying sunscreen last Sunday and how that made me feel, and I wonder how I'll cope with his hands over my back for the night. Well, the evening.

As I slip back into my normal clothes, Emily's jabbering away about the music class she took Issy to this morning and how nice it was to meet with some other mums and dads. I leave the change area and hand the dress to the assistant.

"Go on, Val." Emily's enthusiasm is almost contagious. "Keep me online—I want to see what you choose."

"Perhaps I should shop for you—it could be my birthday present for Boyd." I wiggle my eyebrows, making Emily laugh. I admit, she's making the shopping trip almost bearable.

I head next door and realise it's been ages since I've bought nice lingerie for myself.

"There, there, stop." It's fun guiding Emily through the shop via my phone. "That red lace thong will match your dress beautifully."

Emily's right. I also grabbed a matching bra so I could wear the underwear again. Emily knows I don't mind wearing thongs, and I know how much she hates them.

"What about you, Em? Do you think Boyd would like the leatherette thong?"

"Your brother's not into leather." Emily sounds so matter-of-fact. "But the lacy French knickers behind you—do they come in red?"

They do, and I pick up a pair for my best friend, and after we've said goodbye, I also choose some sexy nightwear for her and, as a joke, some latex underwear for Boyd. Emily had teased that I'd need some sexy nightwear for the upcoming weekend getaway, but I reminded her that

Rhys and I would probably be in separate rooms. I love how she rolls her eyes and tells me I clearly don't know my mother well enough.

I've never really introduced my family to anyone I've dated, and I've definitely never taken anyone from Brisbane home to meet them. I can see why Emily would see this as being such a big deal. For me, though, it's an arrangement, and, as much as I'd like it to be otherwise, I know Rhys is just helping me out.

He probably feels sorry for me or something. It would never work with someone as calm as Rhys. He'd become frustrated at my forgetfulness and complain when I wanted to read just one more chapter.

I dated a guy once who told me I was acting like the book was more interesting than him. It was. Authors can create book boyfriends who appear perfect. Although, I don't just read romance. Last week, I read a detective novel where the main character was an older man, and even then, I appreciated how kind he was to his colleagues, despite knowing how to rough up the serial killer he eventually caught.

My dad and brothers are excellent examples of amazing men. I can now add Ken into the mix, too. Having their example in my family life is a double-edged sword, however. I know there are decent men out there who know how to treat a woman, but at the same time, these guys are family, and I recognise I possibly look at them through rose-coloured glasses.

Emily has gotten better at complaining about Boyd. For years, she ignored things that irritated her, but marriage counselling helped her see that he's not perfect, something she reminds me of regularly. It's hard for me to see how a guy might look past my flaws, especially when no one's been able to do so in the past.

I pick up the dress from the boutique next door. It's been hung in a special carrier so it won't crush on the flight to Cassowary Point. The afternoon has gone better than I thought it would, and I wonder how much of that is a carryover from my lunch with Rhys. He has a way of settling me and putting me at ease.

When I get home, I hang my dress in my room. I'm reading the instructions for the bra stickers the assistant sold me when my phone beeps with a message.

RHYS

How was shopping?

> Good. I got a dress and these strange stickers that are meant to keep my tits up. I'm not sure if they'll work or not, so be prepared to catch one escaping on the night.

RHYS

...

I hope he's not typing an essay. The message was seen as soon as I sent it, so there's no point trying to delete it.

RHYS

Sounds intriguing.

> Maybe. I still need shoes, so I will have to head back to the shops over the weekend. Have I told you how much I hate shopping?

RHYS

I need new shoes, too. Weather is looking good tomorrow—want to come sailing again?

> Sounds lovely. Want to come to the shops with me on Sunday?

RHYS

Lock it in. See you, what, tenish again?

> I'm looking forward to it, but I haven't baked a cake.

RHYS

Your presence will be enough, I promise.

> See you then.

We've been having these little text conversations all week. I scroll back at the one from last night and see that it went on for over an hour.

Rhys sent me a couple of memes that his sister had sent him, and I haven't laughed so much at something on my phone for ages.

Conversation with Rhys is easy, be it in person or through a phone. I haven't trusted myself to call him, because I'll probably embarrass him by asking what he's wearing or something. He mentioned the other night that he doesn't enjoy talking on the phone, and I need to respect that, especially if I don't want him running a mile before the gala.

I pour myself a glass of wine and make my way onto the deck, the same place Rhys and I shared dinner last week. It's hard to think it was just a week ago. I feel like I've known him forever. Sure, we work together, but it's not like we've ever spent a lot of time together before now.

I haven't had time to forget anything around Rhys yet, but it will happen. I'm getting better at checking for things before I leave somewhere, be it a plane or taxi, but my mind is usually racing at a thousand miles per hour, and some things simply skip my attention.

I'm much more organised around work. I've never lost a file or left one somewhere it shouldn't be. It's almost like there's work mode Val and non-work mode Val, and in non-work mode, it's free rein to see what will skip my mind.

This weekend will be spent with Rhys. If we were really dating, I'd stay with him Saturday night and then we'd go shopping together. There's electricity when we touch, albeit innocently, and I can only imagine how that would translate to sex. Although that will never happen.

It's a choppy day on the water, but we've still come out, and we find ourselves in the middle of the ocean. I'm not sure how we've gotten so far away from land, but I'm glad there's no chance anyone can see me.

With every rock of the boat, Rhys thrusts deeper inside me. It's like he's matching the rhythm decreed by nature, and my body is not complaining. It's just happened, and I'm really enjoying the ride. I wish I got a good look at his cock before he sank into me, but it feels amazing, stretching me. I can't remember if he put a condom on, but I have my IUD.

I should have put sunscreen on my chest. It's going to get burnt and then possibly fade to a tan that will be darker than the rest of me. I'm going to look like a freak, but no one should be able to tell. I hope it doesn't show when I'm wearing my gown to the gala. Even if it does, I'll be able to think back to this moment.

"Fuck, you feel amazing," Rhys pants as he continues his thrusts. It's suddenly more choppy, and his thrusts have become more frantic. "I love fucking this tight pussy. It's mine, remember, mine only. No more guys from bars or idiots who don't know what they're doing. Remember, from now on, this pussy belongs to me."

There's something about Rhys' words that sees a further wave of arousal envelop me. I can hear my moans, but I can't say anything, as I'm simply too aroused. It's never been like this. Never felt so damn good.

Rhys bites on a breast, swirling his tongue over the mound, but ignoring the sensitive nipple. "These should be pierced. Imagine the feeling of me tugging on the bar with my teeth, adding to your pleasure."

I've contemplated piercing my nipples in the past, but never managed to get it done. If Rhys is keen, then I am, too.

"You," I groan. "Your cock. Same."

I'm making little sense, but it's no surprise when I'm being thoroughly fucked like this.

"You pierce your gorgeous titties, I'll pierce my cock. What, a Prince Albert, Jacob's ladder? Even an apadravya so I can scrape along your inner walls and give you more pleasure."

I've never been with a guy with a piercing before, but the thought that someone would do it to increase my pleasure astounds me. I'm not surprised that this is something Rhys would consider. My orgasm is so close, but it also feels distant. I'm trying to chase it, but it keeps running away, telling me I need to work for it.

It's not fair. If Rhys comes before me and doesn't make any effort to continue until I've found my pleasure, I'll have to set him free. It's my number one rule, after all, and I don't want to do that. I want to continue and see where else we can go. There's something wet splashing my face. Has he pulled out, and he's coming on my face like a porn star? It's not something we talked about, and I'm not ready for him to not be inside me anymore.

"No!" I scream as I jerk upwards, only to find Rhys standing over me, a towel in hand.

*What the fuck is happening?*

# 10

# Rhys

I think I'm drooling when Val arrives at the boat. I don't recognise her at first when she strolls down the jetty wearing a red-and-white striped T-shirt and the shortest navy shorts I've seen in ages. A large floppy sunhat covers her head, held down by her hand, as it looks like it will fly away on the breeze. It's the patent red high heels that get me, though. She wobbles as she walks, clearly not used to them, but they do the job of making my cock rock hard as my imagination drifts to images of her legs wrapped around me wearing only those shoes.

"Hello, Sailor." Her hip pops as she stands in front of *Serenity*.

"Good God, woman, what the fuck are you wearing?" I've never seen Val like this and wonder if I have indeed misjudged her, and she really is like all the other women who'd tried to chase me.

"It's my boating outfit, Captain," she says as she purses her lips, lips covered in a rich red lipstick that I want to see smeared around my cock. Her tone changes as she stands up straight. "Seriously though, I brought a change of clothes, but I wanted to see your face. It really is priceless."

She takes off the hat and runs her fingers through her short hair before shoving it in her oversized tote bag and replacing it with the company cap she wore last weekend.

"Don't laugh." I shake my head as I smile. "I invited this woman on here once, I mean, we'd been on a couple of dates, and she told me she loved sailing, and she turned up just like that, with the heels included, except her T-shirt was a little more, um, cropped, and she thought she'd just laze on the bow in her bikini all day. Of course, she got seasick, and we headed back to port half an hour after we left, and I never saw her again."

Val removes her shoes, and I hold out a hand to help her on board. My breath almost hitches as our hands touch. I hope she feels the electric current that seems to pass between us, too.

"I'm surprised you aren't married, partnered, settled, or whatever already. You really are a bit of a catch." Val covers the T-shirt with a white-collared blouse that covers both her neck and arms. It hides the curves shown with her shirt, but to me, it makes her more alluring. It's the practicality, the need to be herself, and seeing her comfortable in the practical clothes she chose to wear makes me want her more.

"I've had a couple of serious girlfriends, both of which married the next guy that came along. See, that should give you hope. After the sixteenth, you'll meet the man you'll end up marrying." I try to sound upbeat, but the thought of this being over after Valentine's Day is a reality I don't want to face yet. I know friendship with Val would never be enough.

I'm not lying when I tell her about my serious girlfriends, but they were never serious enough for me to consider forever with them.

"I doubt that. I don't know if I'm choosy or what. Sure, I have no trouble attracting men, and I still pick up when I need to, but I don't know..." Val shrugs her shoulders as she sits down to put on her sneakers.

"You are an incredibly beautiful woman. I mean, I get that you get to deal with terrible relationships every day, but doesn't it also show you what makes a good partnership?" I ask, moving away, as I don't trust myself not to reach out and touch her.

Val pauses, tying her laces before she looks at me. "I suppose." She shrugs. "I mean, the number of people I deal with who can't communicate their needs effectively, plus, I know I wouldn't do cheaters. I understand I have a pretty high sex drive, but I have toys I use fairly regularly, and I'd never consider looking elsewhere if my partner wasn't around or something. Not that I've ever done long-distance or anything, but... Sorry, I'm rambling."

I could listen to her ramble all day. I wish she didn't have to resort to toys, though, and could use me. Fuck, I'd let her use me any way she wished, knowing Val's the sort of woman who would give as good as she got. I love that she has few inhibitions about sex. Maggie would adore her, and I know she'd get on well with Myf.

My cock is so hard, and I'm glad Val unties the ropes, allowing me to hide behind the wheel, and we head out of the marina. There are quite a few vessels out today. Soon, the sails are hoisted, and the wind takes us in the opposite direction from last weekend. Val sits next to me at the helm as we enjoy the feel of gliding over the water. There really is nothing like it.

"My parents are swingers," I say very matter-of-factly.

I haven't planned on telling Val, but Myf is on about dinner tomorrow night and bringing Val to meet Maggie and Tom next weekend.

"Is that an inherited trait?" she asks, seemingly not perturbed by my revelation.

"Good God, no," I gasp, shaking my head. "My last relationship ended because she found someone else, and she couldn't understand why I didn't want him in our bed, too." I don't add that I never saw a future with Lindy. She was nothing more than a warm body, really, but the idea of watching someone else fuck her didn't excite me.

"My last boyfriend was controlling." Val's legs stretch out in front of her. She hasn't changed out of the navy shorts, and I'm not complaining. Her legs go on for miles. "We met in a bar. I thought it might be cool to date a tradie. He was a sparky, you see. I got extra power points installed through the cottage, so that was a bonus, I suppose."

Val sounds like she misses him as she talks about this guy, but I suspect she misses being in a relationship. I can't see anyone controlling Val as she clearly is her own woman, and I want to tell her how I'll always encourage and support her. Perhaps she wants to be controlled in the bedroom. Shit. I could try that. It seems a little un-Val-like though. I mean, I'll always make sure she's satisfied, be it in or out of the bedroom. But maybe I'm boring. I'm quiet and reserved. Maybe I wouldn't be enough for her. I want to ask her more about her sexual preferences, but she opens her mouth to ask more questions.

"So, tell me about your parents, then. Did they just come out and tell you they swing?" Val looks at me, and I can see there's no judgement in her eyes. I told one girlfriend years ago about this, and she basically ran away from our date.

"Not exactly." I shake my head as I remember the night I discovered my parents' lifestyle preferences. "When I was sixteen, I was staying at a friend's place overnight. I'd forgotten a charging cable, so I thought I'd stop off at home for it. I walked into the lounge to find my father balls deep in my English teacher, whilst his wife was eating out my mother."

"Jesus Christ. That would be enough to scar a kid for life." Val doesn't giggle or look disgusted. She places her hand on my arm as if she's concerned for me.

"Yeah. I can laugh about it now, but it was a surprise, that's for sure." It feels different telling Val. Her actions tell me she doesn't think less of me because my parents aren't necessarily conventional. "So, yeah. Maggie identifies as bi, and Tom as pan. That was a lovely dinner conversation."

"My parents are demonstrative in their love for each other and don't care who's listening, but we've never really talked about their sexuality around the dinner table." She's contemplative as she looks to the distance. "I mean, when Henry came out, Dad just asked if someone could pass the salt. It led to a declaration by Giles and Boyd that they thought they were straight, and I told them all that sex was disgusting. I mean, I was, what, nine."

I tell Val about how Tom and Maggie have always hated being called Mum and Dad and how I never knew my grandparents. She hears stories of me distracting the police as a fifteen-year-old whilst Tom hid the few tubs of marijuana he had growing behind the house. Pot was illegal at the time, and the police really only cared about commercial quantities. Tom had always said that Uncle Derek would get him off, anyway.

It's strange to reminisce about my parents' relationship with my father's brother. They almost accepted that he was a criminal defence barrister and argued that he 'stuck it to the man' in getting people off who had been wrongly arrested. Their views of law and order still are quite free, and they argue most people who are arrested are being persecuted by the authorities, except if they have terrorised children. That's their hard limit.

They see me as a soft cock for going into maritime law. I look corporate. I may not have married, which they believe is a win, but I don't have dreads like Myf, or my ear pierced. Val's right, and I am almost refined.

I glance over at Val, and she's drifted off to sleep. I can see why. It's gentle out here today, and I'm not looking for any wind to take us anywhere. We swam after lunch again, but I didn't get to hold her or be close to her like last weekend. There was no current to drift her away from the boat this time and instead, we both simply cooled off.

She looks so peaceful, resting like she is. I throw in a line and tug my hat further down to protect my face from the sun's harsh rays. Val is in some shade, and I know she reapplied sunscreen when we got out of the water.

Almost an hour has passed, and my guest is still asleep. I hear the motorboats in the distance before I see them. They won't miss us with the large sail up, but they are chopping up the water. *Serenity* bobs about. I pull in my lines, knowing there'll be no fish biting now.

Val looks like she's mumbling something, but I can't make out her words. I think I hear her moan. The boats are racing each other and one is heading closer to us. *Pricks*. I see motorboat riders as men in flash sports cars. They're overcompensating for a lack of something somewhere, and usually it's more than a lack of brains.

Reaching for a towel, water sprays onto the deck, hitting us both. Val jerks awake, yelling, "No!"

"It's just some idiots in motorboats." I pass her the towel as she wipes the spray from her face. "You looked so peaceful there for a while."

Val's cheeks redden as she folds the towel and lies it on her knee. "I was dreaming."

If it's anything like the dreams I've been having, I can imagine why she's blushing. Val oozes sexuality, but I don't think she sees it. I feel like I'm constantly turned on just by being in her presence.

"I'm not sure how I'll survive not coming out on *Serenity* after our contract is over." Once again, Val looks out to sea and I can't see her face. Her voice is gentle, almost wistful.

"You're an excellent guest, and I'll happily bring you out whenever you want." I try not to sound too enthusiastic. The thought that Val wants to be here is something.

"I just, I mean, I..." Val lets out a breath. "I don't want people thinking we're more than friends. I know I made a spectacle of myself this morning in that outfit, but a couple of people around the marina seemed to recognise me and said hello, and I definitely don't want people at work to know I see you socially."

"You see Janet socially." I try not to sound defensive.

"Yeah, but everyone knows about Penny, and they don't see me as chasing after her. I've had male friends before, but, well, not from work. I have rules I try to guide my relationships with. One is that he has to give me an orgasm if there's a chance of us getting naked together for a second time, and another is I don't date anyone from work, and that extends to anyone I might come up against in a courtroom."

I feel like I'm back where I started. Val is firmly placing me in the friend zone. I shouldn't complain. It's what I signed up for. For me, though, I can see us working so well together, both in and outside our careers. Her family are all doctors married to doctors, and she complains she doesn't want to date a doctor, but she also doesn't want to date a lawyer either. Well, she doesn't want to date me.

"So, no lawyers, no doctors?" I ask, my nose scrunched up in disbelief.

"When I worked at Legal Aid, there was a workplace romance that went bad. It just ruined the atmosphere in the entire office," Val explains. "I know it sounds odd seeing we work with Max and Katherine, and knowing my family's fascination with all things medical, but I've had to create this rule for me to stop me from causing havoc and needing to change jobs every few months."

Val would be the last person to intentionally cause havoc in any workplace. She jokes about her forgetfulness, but she remembers the important things like appointments and court hearings, and she's told me the dates of all the birthdays in her large family. I've had bills that have skipped my attention before. I actually think Val hides behind her perceived forgetfulness as a way she thinks others will find undesirable.

Val needs someone who can challenge her intellect. It's clear none of the losers she's dated before came close to doing this. She loves family law and is incredible at it, but I wonder how much has influenced her views of family and happily ever afters. Perhaps she needs to meet Maggie and Tom and see that two people can live together for almost forty years and not be married.

It took me a long time to reconcile their lifestyle with their commitment to each other and to Myf and me. Maggie laughed the time I asked if Tom was really our father or if there was another man out there who had knocked up our mother. She explained that she and my father are totally committed to each other, but they also like spreading their love to others. I've got no idea if they have regular play partners, or if they still see my former teacher and his wife or not, but they're definitely committed to each other and their family, no matter how different it looks from what I imagine the Hartman family looks like.

We're going shopping tomorrow. I won't ask Val to come to dinner to meet Myf. As much as I want to spend all the time in the world with this woman, she has made it clear that she can't see a relationship forming between us, and I need to respect that. I want to spend all the time I can with her, but I also need to protect myself.

"It's Tom's birthday next week and Myf, Rob, and I were thinking of heading down for lunch on Sunday. You'd be welcome to join us. It's a pleasant drive, and there are lots of little pop-up stalls on the sides of the road that sell anything from honey to pecans. Plus, my sister wants to meet you." I look out at the water as I talk, worried Val will not agree to this excursion.

"Should I be worried about Myf wanting to meet me? She knows about the arrangement, I assume?" Val bites her bottom lip and furrows her brow.

"No, not at all. Rob's been talking about how amazing you are to work with," I chuckle.

"Jesus. She wants to poke my eyes out and thinks I'm after him or something?" Val has her eyes closed now and throws her head forward into her hands.

"No." I shake my head. "She's met Melinda and Sandy, and Katherine and Max, of course, but hasn't met you."

Val sits upright and gazes out at the water for a while, and I can almost see the thoughts running through her head. Eventually, she looks over at me.

"Look, I know your mum's a baker and all, but would she like me to bake a cake?" Val asks quietly.

"She'd love that. I'll tell her. Hey, thanks for those books, by the way. I enjoyed them all. I really loved this one. The ending was not what I was expecting, but it was so satisfying." I pass Val the pile I had stowed in a locker under my seat.

"I know, right? I mean, she was so badass."

"She reminded me of you." I smile.

"No way." Val shakes her head. "I'd forget to pack bullets or something, and I don't know if I could actually shoot anyone like she did. The language, though, and the description of her doing a no-handed cartwheel whilst she shot four guys and dodged the bullet that was destined for her head. Wow."

I love how animated Val gets.

It's dark by the time we dock. It's been another gorgeous day spent with Val. Staying out in the bay watching the sunset was beautiful. Seeing the colours reflect off the water on Val's face made me wish I was an artist and could capture the image forever. I snapped a photo without her knowing, though. If a picture can tell a thousand words, it describes her beauty better than any thesaurus could manage. She may have placed me in the friend zone, but at least she hasn't dismissed me altogether.

If I only get these few weeks with Val, it will be an experience that will live with me forever. Maybe I'll end up like Uncle Derek and not spend my life with anyone.

"Can you walk in them?" I'm with Val as she tries on shoes.

"Yeah, but I don't think I could dance in them. You dance, I hope. I hadn't thought to ask before now." Val looks in the mirror, oblivious to how the shoes make her leg muscles flex in all the right places.

"I love dancing. It's my dream to find the perfect woman who will want to dance with me on the deck of our boat as the sun sets." The words are out before I can stop them.

After Val left last night, I spent ages trying to relax. I put on some slow jazz and actually fantasised about dancing with her on deck in the middle of the ocean. My cock swells in my jeans as it remembers the three times I climaxed, and even then it wasn't satisfied. I knew nothing would ever happen with her, and I'd have to find a way to stop this, but not just yet.

I'd blacked out the sixteenth of February in my diary knowing this is our supposed end date. We'd have a wonderful weekend together. Her family would be convinced we were the real deal, and I'd have to come home and pretend like nothing happened. Yet I can't escape the feeling that something wonderful could happen between us if only Val would let go of her rules. I sigh inwardly as I lament the predicament I find myself in.

I need to admit that this will not go anywhere, and I just focus on playing my part to help Val out. I'm confused. I'm infatuated with the woman. Fuck, I think I might even be in love with her.

"If only you'd told me last night; we could have danced then." Val grips my arm as she wobbles in the shoes. As much as I would have loved her to wear them and have her needing to hold on to me for the evening, they are pretty impractical.

In the end, Val settles for a lovely pair of gold shoes that are not too high to prevent dancing, and yet are high enough to stop her dress dragging on the floor. Well, that's how she justified them, anyway.

As we shop for shoes for me, Val tells me all about Ken's love of shiny shoes, and she snaps photos of several pairs that she thinks he'd love.

I loved Val has this relationship with her brothers and their partners. I'm lucky I get on well with Rob. He's the perfect secretary, even if he should be an author. Indeed, if he plods along and only writes a few words per week, he'll get there. He probably is writing a bestseller.

After trying on several pairs of dressy shoes, I settle for a pair I can also wear to work.

"It's your practicality shining through." Val laughs.

She said she doesn't care what I wear at all. Unlike previous girlfriends who'd wanted me to wear the latest fashions and insisted that I had to complement their wardrobes, Val doesn't give a damn. It might be because we're only playing at this, but I get the impression that external image isn't high on Val's priority list.

We're heading towards a café for lunch when I hear our names being called.

"Rhys, Valerie. What are you two doing out together? I never realised, but it makes a lot of sense. Go for it, you two." Katherine doesn't let either of us get a word in as she kisses us both on our cheeks.

I squeeze Val's arm as she freezes in place, not having expected to bump into anyone we know. "Katherine, I am just Val's plus one for a family event in a couple of weeks, that's all."

"Ah, there you are, darling." Katherine looks around for her husband, who is carrying a bag of books. It reminds me that perhaps Val and I need to visit the bookshop after lunch. "Max, Rhys is trying to tell me he and Val aren't an item, and we're just going along with it, okay? Aren't they just perfect together?"

"I know not to question my wife after forty-something years, but Val, Rhys, it is lovely seeing you both. Will you join us for lunch?" Max grips my hand firmly in a greeting as Katherine starts walking, her arm in Val's. Val glances at me walking behind her, and it appears neither of us are prepared to speak. "Good. That settles it then. Have you been to the café down this alleyway? Val, do you remember when you first started, Anton Greenway, his wife, had all those affairs and only married him for his money..."

Val nods. I'm so glad she's had Katherine's tutorage over the years.

"He was a restaurateur, Rhys, and had a string of successful businesses. It was Val's recommendation to him to put the child on the Federal Police list to not allow him to leave the country, which was fortunate, if I recall correctly." Katherine hardly takes a breath. "Anyway, the ex-wife was a bitch, and, in the end, the child chose to live with him. He's remarried, and his wife had a baby a few months ago, and he now runs this little café down here."

It was a delicious lunch. Anton had indeed remembered Val, and she seemed embarrassed when he again told her how she was always one step ahead of what his ex had planned. We were introduced to his lovely wife and baby son. His daughter, Marianna, was our waitress for the day too.

"Katherine, Val, thank you again. You saved me more than I can ever repay and, as you can see, Selina is just beautiful and perfect, and Marianna is the most amazing young woman. She wants to study law, too."

"So, what's different this time?" Max asks, taking a keen interest in the new relationship.

Anton is quick to reply. "I didn't settle for less than I wanted. I settled the first time around when she did not tick every box. We didn't communicate well. I wanted more children, and she didn't. This time, it took a while for me to accept that it was right, but I'm so glad I did. Selina's perfect."

"No, I'm not." Selina shakes her head, a smile on her face. She happily accepts her husband's arm as it wraps around her waist and places her head on his shoulder. "He portrays me as this saint for taking him and Marianna on, but really, he is the perfect one. I mean, he's an absolute tiger in the bedroom, and I have no idea why his first wife needed to look elsewhere."

We all laugh, and Val and I catch each other's glances, both looking at each other when we think the other isn't watching.

As we are preparing to go our separate ways, Katherine reminds us Valentine's Day is coming up. "I got a sneaky little something for Max this morning. My advice to you two is not to let the romance die."

Katherine was off before I could remind her that Val and I aren't a couple, and if Val has her way, we never will be.

"Do you think she'll talk at work?" Val asks as she plays with the handles on the bag carrying her new shoes.

"No." I shake my head. "She'll wiggle her eyebrows at me, but that won't be new. Katherine's never been a gossip. Did you want to swing by a bookshop before heading home?"

"No." Val shakes her head. "I've told my books at home that they aren't getting any new friends until I've read ten of them. I've still got eight to go. Did you get that Kindle?"

"No." I roll my eyes. "I got distracted by the books that are available and started a wishlist or something."

"That sounds like something I'd do." Val chuckles as we head towards the car park we met at this morning. "I need to get home to bake. I want to try out a new chocolate cake recipe, and if it is acceptable in the office tomorrow, I'll bake one to take to meet your parents."

I loved the way Val talked about meeting my parents. I knew it wasn't as my girlfriend, and I'd be introducing her as a friend, but it still gave me a very satisfied feeling inside.

"We probably should have a little something to give each other for Valentine's, or at least a story for my parents, as there's no doubt they'll ask us," Val suggests as we reach the lift that will take us to our cars.

"Let's surprise each other. It doesn't have to be big, but I can think of the perfect little something for you." I hoped Val recognised the smile that spread all over my face was put there by her, and her alone.

11

# Val

IT'S THE SCIENCE OF BAKING THAT I LOVE, THE WAY YOU CAN cream butter and sugar, add eggs, flour, and flavouring, throw it in the oven, and something amazing comes out. When I'm not reading, I'm usually searching for new cake recipes. I love how different countries have their own take on all things cake and how these have evolved as the world grew smaller.

Mum has hundreds of cookbooks. I suspect she has many she's never cooked a recipe from. One of my favourite cake recipes comes from a ninety-nine-cent book I remember Mum and I picking up at a discount bookstore that had popped up in Cassowary Point one holiday season. German Plum Cake, although I'm not sure how authentically German it is.

The sight of nectarines in the produce section reminds me of another cake I love to bake. I grab some of the sweet-smelling fruit and some yoghurt, and I know I'll bake one of these for my colleagues. They didn't get a cake last week, so they can have two tomorrow.

As much as I love the process of traditional baking with creaming fat and sugar, I'm always intrigued by other methods. During the week, I stumbled across a buttermilk chocolate cake with chocolate cream cheese frosting. The photo online made it look so decadent. Rhys loved the cake I baked last weekend. I was in two minds, suggesting I take a cake for his father's birthday, but Rhys was encouraging, and I decided to give the new chocolate cake a go.

It's an all-in-one cake, meaning only one bowl, which I appreciate. The batter has that lovely balance of bitter from the chocolate and sweet from the sugar, and if it is as moist as the blogger suggests, then it should be rich and decadent.

Placing the cake pans in the oven and closing the door, I turn to the benches and clean up the chocolate cake so I can prepare the ingredients for the nectarine one. It's been a while since I've done a baking spree like this. I know I'm doing it to keep myself busy and my mind from wandering to Rhys and our day on the water yesterday.

Rhys has opened up so much over the last couple of weeks, and it's given me much more insight into him. I had to put my foot down, though, and set some boundaries before I got swept away by the chemistry of it all, and there is definite chemistry between us. He's exactly the type of guy I can see myself falling for. Not only is he exceptionally good-looking, but he's a thinker. Even though his mind is so sharp, he's not an intellectual snob.

I feel heard by him. It's not just me, though. At the retreat weekend, I saw how he was with our other colleagues. He's attentive and inquisitive. Janet told me during the week that he's making a point of helping Melinda as she prepares to leave her horrible marriage. Perhaps it shouldn't surprise me that Rhys is a hit with all of our colleagues. He's shown he can be supportive and friendly towards them, and so, I have to believe we, too, can be friends, despite what my body might otherwise believe, especially after *that* dream on his boat.

Janet was in meetings most of last week, and I didn't get to update her on how well Rhys and I are getting along. Maybe if I was friendly with any of my exes, I'd be more willing to investigate some form of relationship with Rhys, even if it's just sex until we come back from Cassowary Point, but that would break my no fraternisation at work policy.

I wipe the counter before washing my hands. In my mind, I can't differentiate horniness from pure desire for Rhys and whether the two are indeed one and the same. It will make selling our relationship to my family that much easier.

The dream on *Serenity* threw me. When Rhys woke me, I hoped I hadn't been vocal whilst I slept. He didn't question anything, but it reminded me that there was no way we could go back to being colleagues after a sexual relationship. Away from his shyness, Rhys gives off protective energy that I think would translate well into the bedroom. It's the sort of energy I don't think anyone would want to give up. I notice my bottom lip between my teeth as I worry that my brain may catch up to my body, a body that clearly appreciates the satisfaction it knows Rhys would provide.

It was strange bumping into Katherine and Max in the city this morning. Rhys was adamant we weren't together, and although that's what I told him I wanted, it still feels disappointing to hear. *God, I'm so indecisive.* I know why Rhys and I can't form a relationship, and I need to stick to the reasons. A dalliance would be a disaster.

After mixing the ingredients for the second cake, I slice nectarines and can almost imagine Rhys feeding me slivers of fruit. My nipples pebble at the thought. I place the fruit decoratively on the bottom of the pan and spoon the batter on top, careful to not dislodge the pattern I've created.

The timer on my phone chimes, and I check the cakes in the oven. They seem to be cooked, so I remove them before placing the nectarine cake in and resetting the timer. I'm stacking the dishwasher when my phone rings. The tone is the one I set for Emily's FaceTime calls.

"Hey. It's not that time already, is it?" I ask as Mia grabs the phone from Emily.

"Auntie Val!" Mia shrieks, her smile almost wider than her face, and I can tell she's bouncing on her feet. "Is your boyfriend there? I want to see him. Dad says you're smitten."

"I did not say smitten, Mia!" Giles yells from out of the shot of the camera.

"You did, too, Dad," Millie rebuffs him.

"Hello everyone." I laugh. "No, Rhys isn't here. He has dinner with his sister and her husband on Sunday evenings when he can."

"Well, why aren't you there?" Mia's brows knit, and she rolls her eyes just like a Hartman.

"We spent yesterday together on his boat, Mia, and then we went shopping this morning." I can't believe I'm defending myself to an eleven-year-old.

"What did he cook for breakfast?" Boyd pokes his head around Mia and waves at me. "Cream pies?"

"Boyd Edward Abraham Hartman." Oooh, Emily's full named him, which makes me laugh.

"Mum says you can't have pie for breakfast." Millie is still off screen.

"Are you back at school?" I ask Mia, knowing the new year started last week.

She tells me all about being a senior in her primary school and how she's been elected music captain.

"I was school captain in grade six." I can almost hear Millie's eye roll as she reminds her sister of her achievements.

Millie tells me about grade eight and how boring it is. Boyd teases her about Troy, a boy in her class who seems to have taken a fancy to her.

Mum comes on the line and tells me about the gala preparations, and Dad asks me to help him with a crossword clue. Millie solves it before I have a chance to open my mouth. I'm passed back and forth between members of my family, hearing how their week has been and telling them about sailing yesterday.

The time chimes on my phone, and I check on the cake.

Henry grabs the phone from Mia. "Ooh, what is it this week?" I can see him almost drooling.

"This one's the nectarine and yoghurt cake I love, and I've also tried a new chocolate cake, a triple layer all-in-one number with chocolate cream cheese frosting."

"What's the occasion?" Ken peers at the cakes I'm showing them and lets out a low moan.

"It's Rhys' dad's birthday next weekend, and we're going down to see them. I said I'd take cake, and I wanted to try out a new one. Plus, the nectarines looked great, so why not?" I shrug.

"No one bakes me a birthday cake," Dad grumps in the background.

"I'll bring you cake, Dad, when I come up for the gala."

"Your mother used to bake every weekend." Dad sounds sullener than usual.

"Yes, and then your colleague and best friend had to have that quadruple bypass, and you decided to make some lifestyle changes. You've been doing so well with your cycling." Mum grabs the phone and plants a kiss on Dad's cheek. He may sound grumpy, but I'm glad to see he's all smiles.

"So, you're getting leg muscles, Dad?" I ask as I switch off the oven and move outside to the deck.

"Ooh, yes," Mum coos. "Still no upper body definition, but legs of steel. They can—"

"Mum!" I hear Giles and Boyd yell in unison.

I feel so far away from them all.

It's great that they still involve me by having this weekly video chat, but it doesn't make up for me not being there to soothe Issy when she's fussing, or give Dad a hug, or bake him a cake.

Bridget's holding Issy, and Millie's reading her a story. The story is War and Peace, which Millie has decided she is ready to tackle. Even I haven't read that one. Henry boasts about a catch Ken took at a cricket game yesterday.

I look at them all so loved up and happy. That's not on the cards for me. The men I've dated have all told me I'm too intense. If I've got a big case, it's not uncommon for me to put in fifty or sixty hours at work in a week to make sure everything's ready to go and we have the best argument we can present to a judge.

I've also been open with the guys I've dated in telling them that my long-term goal is to move back to Cassowary Point to be near my family. I might as well have told some guys I was moving to Antarctica.

The phone is finally passed to Bridget after everyone else appears to have tired from talking to me. Ken, Henry, and Dad are back in the kitchen getting dinner ready. Mia's playing something on the piano, and Emily, Boyd, and Mum are listening. Millie is back reading to herself, and Issy's playing with Bridget's necklace.

"Is everything okay with you and Rhys?" Bridget is bouncing Issy on her lap.

"Of course." I know I sound defensive. I should have remembered we had a family call this evening, but it had slipped my mind as I didn't put it on my calendar.

"I'm surprised you aren't with him and his sister this evening, that's all."

Fuck.

"We spent yesterday and half of today together." I smooth out my voice, hoping to appear calmer than I feel. I can't stuff this up now. "Plus, we work together, so we need some time apart."

"That's true." Bridget takes a sip of water from the glass in front of her. "Just don't self-sabotage it."

I don't answer that. When I first moved to Brisbane, I lived with Giles and Bridget. I remember at the time Bridget telling me I was so much like my oldest brother, it was scary, but I needed to work out, as he had done, that commitment wasn't necessarily scary.

As a seventeen-year-old, I rolled my eyes, but almost thirteen years later, perhaps her counsel back then had merit. Maybe I need to set out to find someone who wants the same things as me, someone who can put up with my crazy schedule and idiosyncrasies. Someone who can more than tolerate me, but maybe love me. It doesn't have to lead to marriage, but if it's someone I can see myself getting along with in the long run, then I might have a child. If I choose the right person, surely we will be able to co-parent successfully.

Of course, this imaginary person would need to want to move to Cassowary Point or put up with seeing their child less frequently. Maybe it would have been better to go to the gala alone and see if I can meet Mr Right, just like Henry did ten years ago.

No matter what happens, I know my family will support me, even if I make crazy and inappropriate decisions. Just like the one I've gotten myself into with Rhys.

"Okay, which one's yours?" Janet storms into my office Monday morning with two slices of cake on a plate and a cup of tea in her hand. She bumps the door closed with her behind and props herself at my desk before producing two forks.

"Which do you prefer?" I ask as I take a forkful of the chocolate cake. It's divine.

"I recognise the nectarine cake, because you've baked it before, but this chocolate cake..." Janet moans as she licks the frosting from the fork.

"It's good, isn't it?" I try another forkful. "I actually baked them both."

"The chocolate Guinness cake is still a winner, and the chocolate, orange, and almond cake, but this is something else."

"It's Rhys' dad's birthday next weekend, and I said I'd take a cake." I try the nectarine cake, and it's got a lovely crumb, but it's a totally different style of cake to the chocolate one.

"Wait, so you're meeting his parents?" Janet's fork stops in midair, halfway to her mouth.

"It's no big deal." I shrug.

"Um, yeah it is." Janet chuckles. "He's taking you to meet the hippies that no other woman has met."

"I'm going as a friend, though, not a girlfriend, or partner, or anything."

"Does Rhys know that?" Janet lifts her brows and tilts her head.

"Of course. We talked about it on Saturday, and he knows I don't date anyone from work, and we can only be friends."

Janet makes a noncommittal sound that is not a grunt nor a laugh but shows she doesn't agree with me.

A call comes through from a client, so she leaves me to it.

In the end, she could have stayed, as it was a quick call telling me nothing new. I think the client simply sought some reassurance that she was doing the right thing and not rolling over for her ex-husband. I know I'd never roll over in a relationship and let someone else dictate my future, but I've seen men who do this, and they do it well. They manage to subtly question things until their partners can only see their side.

Sure, it's gaslighting, but it's so insidious that, sometimes, even the smartest women don't see it happening.

My client is a successful businesswoman who conducts multi-million dollar deals in the workplace, and yet had a man at home telling her what she was doing was wrong. And now he thinks he can have most of her business as part of a divorce settlement. It will not happen on my watch.

With Janet, Rob, Katherine, Max, and, of course, Rhys and I, knowing about our arrangement, that's more than a quarter of the office. I can't have anyone else find out about my deception. It's only meant to be for my family, but it seems to be getting bigger than I'm comfortable with.

After lunch, there's a knock at my door. "Are you busy?" Katherine asks.

"Come in." I smile, standing to give her a hug. "I've always got time for you."

"I wanted to say again how lovely it was bumping into the two of you yesterday." Katherine is all smiles. I indicate for her to sit where Janet sat to interrogate me this morning.

"We're really just friends," I tell her, my brow creased.

"I know." She reaches over and pats my hand. "But give him a chance if he wants one. He's so much like Derek." Katherine shakes her head, an enormous grin on her face as she reminisces. "Derek was very keen on a friend of mine, but, like his nephew, he was quite shy around people he didn't know. By the time he psyched himself up to make a move, she was with someone else."

"How do you and Max manage working and living together?" I blurt out.

"It was a challenge at first, but then again, we worked for rival firms." Katherine crosses her legs as she leans back in the chair. "I never realised he was the one until much later than he did. We were similar, sure, but we set boundaries. Work doesn't come home with us, and home doesn't come to work with us. It's all about communication. I know in our line of work, it's easy to see all the relationships that don't work out, but we also need to remember that there are plenty that do."

Katherine has a point, but I need to maintain the status quo for now, if only for my own sanity. Besides, I've told Rhys we're friends, and he's accepted that. Why should we ruin the good thing we have going on?

I HAVEN'T SEEN Rhys since Sunday. All week, we've crossed like ships in the night at work. I've been in court too much for my liking, and Rhys isn't in the office that much to begin with. We've shared a few text messages, but nothing that wasn't really business related, the business being our arrangement for the gala.

There's no flirting as such, but his messages make me smile. I've chosen the right person for the job next weekend, that's for sure.

"This is Rob, who you know, and my sister, Myf." Rhys introduces us outside my home as they pick me up to drive to Maggie and Tom's.

"Rhys has said only good things." Myf brings me in for a giant hug at my words. I'm glad he grabbed the cake from me when I was locking the front door.

Myf's hair is a mass of blonde dreadlocks tied on top of her head in a purple band. She has several piercings in her ears, as well as an eyebrow piercing and a septum ring. I blush as I recall my dream and wonder if Rhys might indeed be pierced in places I haven't seen yet.

I sit in the back seat with Rhys, the cake between us. Myf tells us about her job as a midwife and some of the crazy requests she gets from parents.

"So, they agreed to come into the hospital for the delivery because it was high-risk." She leans over the back of her seat to look at me as she talks, her face so expressive. "I'd told them they could bring in a choir if they wanted to and that the delivery suite could probably hold about ten people. So, they brought fifteen. And everyone was naked. Her parents, his parents, siblings, friends. Then they wanted me to get naked too, which I refused, not that I have any issues with nudity, but I needed to come and go from the room, and I don't really fancy amniotic fluid, let alone any other bodily fluids, splashing onto my skin."

"Yeah, she would have gone naked if she could," Rob butts in.

"So, the baby's getting distressed, not badly enough to panic, but I know we're heading towards a caesarian. Dad isn't happy, Mum isn't happy, but there are two happy people getting it on in the corner of the room. So, I head out to the nurse's station to phone the obstetrician on call. Next thing, they're pushing the bed down the corridor, everyone still naked, asking me where the operating room is."

I can't wait to share this story with Bridget, although I suspect she's seen it all, too. She probably shares these types of stories around the dinner table on Sundays when I'm not there.

"Is there anything I need to know about Tom and Maggie that Rhys hasn't told me?" I ask Myf.

"Just be prepared for anything." Myf laughs. "They're both batshit crazy."

"First time they met me"—Rob looks at me through the rearview mirror, a wry grin on his face—"Maggie grabbed me by the crotch to see if I would be able to please her little girl."

Okay then. I know my mother can be intense and inquisitive, but I don't think she'd ever go as far as molesting someone.

"Yeah, and she still complains she found nothing." Rhys smiles as he gazes out the window.

"It was the middle of winter, and I'm a grower, not a shower." Rob justifies, and Myf leans over and rests her hand on his thigh.

"Don't worry, I've told Maggie how amazing your cock is. She knows." Myf wiggles her eyebrows at me, and I can't help but laugh.

"Oh yeah, another warning." Rob shakes his head. "Don't drink Tom's ginger beer. It's so potent."

"He calls it truth serum for a reason." Myf laughs. "Perhaps we'll give some to Rhys, and he can really open up."

"I just want to get through this day." Rhys sighs as he shakes his head.

The car's quiet for a bit. Rhys appears anxious about seeing his parents, and I hope I'm not adding to it. I suppose I invited myself along today, but Rhys seemed keen on the idea. I hope he didn't feel he had to say yes. I'm starting to fret and wonder if Rhys has been avoiding me this week at work.

"Oh, come on, bro. Do you want me to rant about bourgeois capitalism and how we live in a nanny state before we get there? You know they aren't directing their rants at you, don't you?" Myf leans her hand over the back of her chair, and Rhys reaches it for a squeeze.

"It just gets a bit much." Rhys removes his glasses and rubs his eyes. "I'm sorry, Val. They can be quite judgemental."

"It's my penance for you putting up with my mother's antics next weekend trying to marry us off and have lots of babies."

"Well, you won't get marriage talk from Maggie and Tom," Rhys chortles.

"Yeah." Rob gently shakes his head from the driver's seat. "They still haven't forgiven Myf and me for having the audacity to succumb to societal pressure and partake in an outdated practice that shackles women to lives that aren't meant for them."

"Rhys told you they've never married, didn't he?" Myf glances back at me, and I nod.

Sometimes, I wonder if I agree with their views on marriage. I see the aftereffects of bad choices all the time. Sure, in this country, people who live together for over twelve months have the same rights as those who are married under the law, but I don't see a lot of common-law marriages or de facto couples in my office for advice.

It's something I've never really reflected on before. Giles and Bridget had a small wedding in the botanic gardens with just family. Boyd and Emily shocked us all and arranged a surprise wedding at Mum and Dad's house. Heaven knows if Henry and Ken will ever tie the knot. They've been engaged for years now, but there's been no wedding talk.

Marriage is more than a piece of paper, though. It's a commitment made by a couple. Marriage appears to be more than finding the person who's a good fit for you, but finding someone who will put in the work to put up with you. I really can't see that happening to me. I'm not as easygoing as my brothers. Plus, any guy who agrees to be with me will know that I know every legal loophole to ensure I get what I'm due if we end up in the divorce courts.

"They might like that you're a divorce lawyer, though, because that will reinforce their views that marriage as a concept is dead." Myf points at Rob, who shakes his head.

"I'd rather see Maggie's face if we tell her Val's a corporate lawyer

who oversees the takeover of smaller businesses by large multinationals."
Rob laughs.

"If you do that, I'll ask you about your book in front of them,"
Rhys snaps at his brother-in-law. "Val, thank you for coming today, and
I really hope we haven't put you off. Maggie and Tom can be, well, a
handful."

"I'm looking forward to it." I lean over and squeeze his hand, his lips
tilting up slightly, but his brow still furrowed.

To break the tension, I talk a bit about my work, hoping that Myf,
Rob, and Rhys have exaggerated Maggie and Tom, but even if they
haven't, it will be a fun afternoon.

# 12

# Rhys

WHAT THE EVER-LOVING HECK WAS I THINKING BRINGING Val to meet my parents? Over the years, I've told myself I've grown to accept who they are, but then I forget about things, like how Maggie molested Rob the first time they met him.

It's never been an issue for me that they've never married. I never found it strange as a child that I had my father's surname, and Myf had my mother's. That was not uncommon in the community we grew up in. It took a few years for me to get my head around their sexuality and their open relationship.

But that life's not for me.

I wouldn't say I'm possessive, but I could never stand by and watch someone else give my partner pleasure. That's my role, and I think I do a pretty good job. There's been no complaints, and I leave most women in a quivering mess when I've finished. I feel the least shy when I'm naked with a woman, trailing my tongue down her body, nibbling at her pulse points, twirling a nipple in my mouth, teasing her clit with either my mouth, fingers, or a toy, and finally sinking my covered cock deep inside her.

Because my cock is always covered. I've never met anyone who I've trusted enough to have unprotected sex with. I told Val I want kids, but

I'm yet to meet anyone with whom I can imagine raising a child together. There's something about Val though that I can see it with her.

It's been months since I've had sex. On the drive down to my parents, I wonder if I'm attracted to Val because I'm seeking sexual release. I mean, I make do with my hand alright, but it's not the same. The thought of having a child with her makes my cock stir. I can't make any sense of it. I've never had this reaction to any other woman.

I probably need to find someone I can fuck and get Val out of my mind. She's placed me firmly in the friend zone, and I need to respect that. I'm not going to cross any boundaries she's set. That's not fair to her, and I need to respect her wishes, even if they are different from mine.

"Should I have brought a gift?" Val whispers as Rob indicates then turns up the long drive to my parents' home.

I try to reassure her. "You've brought cake. We've got a couple of hanging baskets in the back for them from us all. Maggie and Tom love their plants."

If I didn't know any better, I'd think Val is looking for acceptance from Maggie and Tom, even though that makes little sense.

Rob slows the car, and I look to see if there's a chicken on the road or something.

"This is where we usually strip off." Myf starts unbuttoning her shirt, and I can see Rob trying to keep a straight face as he tugs his T-shirt over his head.

"I, um..." Val doesn't hesitate to lift the tank top from her waist, and I get a glimpse of pale pink lace as her bra comes into view.

"Val." I put out my arm to stop her as I shake my head. "They're having a lend of you."

Myf and Rob are laughing hysterically now as Val looks confused. "Sorry." Myf laughs some more as Rob slips his shirt back on again. "I did this to Rob the first time he visited here. Maggie and Tom may be many things, but they aren't usually naturists around us."

It seems I'm the only one in the car not laughing. Val thinks it's a great prank. The fact she would have gone along with it makes me realise again how important she is to me. She didn't question anything, just went to raise her top.

Rob continues up their tree-lined drive. "Nice bra, by the way," I lean across and whisper in her ear. Val's cheeks redden, and I welcome her slap to my arm as the car pulls to a stop.

We're greeted by two dogs with faces only a mother could love, both rescued from the local pound.

"Come here, Buster," Myf greets the larger dog with rubs to his ears, which he tolerates until he rolls onto his back and almost bounces on the ground as he waits for his belly to be ruffled with her foot.

"Down, Woofa." My firm tone does nothing to stop the second dog from jumping all over Val.

Val passes me the container with the cake in it and bends down to pick up the small dog. She loves this and rewards Val with licks to her face, something Val doesn't seem to mind.

"We never had pets growing up." Val scratches behind Woofa's ears, the dog's tail beating a steady rhythm against her stomach. "Dad said four kids were enough. Boyd and Emily have a lovely dog now, though, and one day, I'd love one that I can walk and throw a ball for."

Maggie and Tom appear from the house, and I make introductions. Maggie's a hugger, and I'm almost jealous that she gets to hold Val. We present Tom with the hanging pots, one containing a fern, and the other some succulent that will flower in the next few weeks according to the man at the nursery.

Rob carries them both as Myf and Val walk towards the front of the house with Maggie, each with an arm through hers.

"She seems nice, Rhys," Tom offers as we walk a few meters behind.

"She is." I nod. "But like I said on the phone, she's a friend, and that's it."

Tom pats me on the back, his action saying more than words. He knows I'm infatuated with Val. I suspect everyone except Val is aware.

My parents lived in a shed on this block when they first got together. The shed's still there, but they've since built a pretty impressive house. All the materials are recycled. There's a wastewater system that waters the large vegetable garden they both love and solar panels that allow them to live off grid. I know building it was a community effort, and some of my first memories are of the groups of people who would come and help position girders or sand timber floors when it was all coming together.

And they've never stopped improving it either. The aquaponics system they set up several years ago is going strong, and they now have a large battery bank to store some of the solar energy they don't sell back to the electricity company.

They're on a few acres with chickens and geese, and a flock of ducks has made a home on the large dam at the back of the property. They have two dairy cows which they milk twice a day, Tom loving nothing more than cheese making.

The view from the rear of the house is spectacular. A vista of rolling hills as far as they eye can see is a far cry from the suburban life Val, Myf, and Rob live in, and the water that I call home. Val sits in one of the two chairs my parents use in the evenings. I'm perched on the edge of the verandah, leaning up against a post.

The scene is peaceful, but I'm anything but. My toe taps in my shoe, and I can feel the tension through every inch of my body. I almost jump when Rob rubs my shoulder as he walks past with an assortment of glasses. Maggie's brought out some of their home-brewed kombucha.

"It's non-alcoholic, but I can add some of our ginger beer." Maggie pours a glass and passes it to Val.

"This smells lovely, thanks, Maggie." Val sounds like Maggie is her new bestie, the two of them sitting together, far enough away from me that I can't hear their conversation.

Myf's plonked herself on the ground at Maggie's feet, her back resting against our mother's legs.

"Just friends, my arse." Tom chuckles as he lights whatever leaf he's got rolled in his cigarette papers. The smell tells me it's a combination of tobacco and pot.

"You know that's going to kill you, don't you?" I reply, still staring at the women. Myf and Maggie are laughing, and Maggie has a hand on Val's arm.

"How's work?" Tom takes a long drag and blows the smoke away from us. "Smooth sailing?"

"Good one." Rob chuckles as he throws the ball for Buster, who dutifully retrieves it and returns it to his feet.

"Always busy." My reply is curt.

It's not often that I spend time with my parents. I know I'm the one who brings tension to our meetings, but I feel like I'm an utter disappointment to them. I feel judged. Rob and Myf have told me time and time again that this is a 'me' problem and that I read more into it than is actually there.

"And how's this book coming along, Rob?" Tom stubs out the cigarette on the deck before placing the butt in a jar that is half full of discarded smokes.

"Not much progress, I'm afraid." Rob sighs. "I've hit a snag and have had to investigate different weaponry."

"I still can't see why you don't quit your day job and focus on your writing." Buster has now dropped the ball at Tom's feet, and he throws it much further than Rob managed. It's soon retrieved and returned, only for the process to continue.

"Rhys needs me there to keep him in line, Tom." Rob bumps his shoulder against mine.

"Well, he needs a wingman if he's going to get the woman." Tom retrieves another pre-rolled cigarette from a case, but puts it away when Maggie shoots him a glare.

"Val and I are friends." I shake my head before banging it against the pole I'm leaning against. "I'm helping her out for her family gala next weekend, that's it. Then it finishes. We're back to being colleagues. It's all plotted and planned."

This time next week, we'll be preparing to go our separate ways. My stomach sinks with the realisation. Val is laughing away with Myf and Maggie as if she's known them both for years. Maggie stands, and Myf and Val follow.

"Oh, Rhys." Maggie places her hands on my shoulders, leans down, and kisses the top of my head. "Val's amazing. She's hilarious. Those stories about some of the idiot exes she has to deal with. No wonder you're so taken with her."

"It's an arrangement, Maggie." I close my eyes and take a deep breath, my voice clipped.

"You tell yourself that, son." She pats my shoulder like I'm a small child.

"Oh, no, it is." Val looks appalled that anyone could think otherwise. "I don't date anyone in the office, and as lovely and hot as Rhys is, if we blurred the lines now, it would make it pretty hard in the office when the arrangement is over."

Maggie rolls her eyes as a grin creeps up one side of her face.

We make our way to the side of the house where Maggie and Tom have set up a table for us to eat at. More glasses are filled with flowers and foliage from the garden and dotted along the surface in no set way, with cutlery piled in jars and jugs. There's never been order and arrangement at my parents' dinner table. Once, I would have thought that them doing the bare minimum was them not making an effort, but an effort has been made, even if it's different from how I might do things.

Val and Tom appear, deep in conversation, both carrying platters. Tom's contains meats and cheese, Val's various salad vegetables that I know came direct from the garden here. I feel like I should have offered to help, but the truth is I needed a few minutes to myself.

Introducing Val to Maggie and Tom could have gone either way. On the drive here, I stressed that they'd criticise her work, or blame her for being part of the corporate jungle that exemplifies all that is wrong with the world. Instead, they've hung off her every word and made her feel welcome.

Myf and Rob appear carrying various condiments and some freshly churned butter, followed by Maggie, who carries a basket of freshly baked bread rolls and another pitcher of kombucha. It's an amazing spread. There's no head of the table at Maggie and Tom's. Instead, we sit where we want, and I'm disappointed to not be sitting next to Val.

"So, family law, I hear." Tom butters his bread roll as he turns to face Val, who's sitting next to him.

"That's right." Val places an assortment of food on her plate before licking the thumb that she swiped through the mango chutney on her plate. Her moan rivals any I've heard from the women I've been with before, and I yearn to suck her thumb into my mouth. "So, lots of divorce settlements and custody arrangements. I mean, I also do wills and things."

"We should do a will," Maggie declares from across the table as she waits for the tongs to be passed to her.

It shouldn't surprise me that Maggie and Tom are intestate, but whenever I've asked them about wills in the past, they've always told me it's organised.

"You most definitely should," Val replies as she takes a sip of her tea. "I'm sure Rhys could help you, or I could always whip up something."

"Oh, would you?" Maggie coos, and I have to close my eyes to stop people from seeing the roll. "Perhaps not today, but in a few weeks, you could come back down, or we could come and meet you in your office, you know, take you and Rhys for lunch."

"Sounds great." Val leans over and places her hand on Tom's. "Are you okay with this? I mean, you don't have to, but if you die without a will, the government will charge to work out who's receiving what."

"And I want to keep the government away from our money." Tom chuckles.

"If Val can't do it, I can always help," I add to the conversation.

"Oh, no." Maggie shakes her head. "We'd love to see Val again, wouldn't we, sweet cheeks?"

"Absolutely, buttercup." I squirm as Tom licks the back of his knife. If Val notices, she says nothing.

Talk turns to the rain they've had recently and how the dam is full. Val talks about a few of her clients in a roundabout way, telling us stories that see me crossing my legs, hoping she never gets my balls in a vice like she seems to do to the exes of many of the people she represents.

After the empty platters are cleared away, the cake Val baked is produced. It's seriously one of the best cakes I've ever tasted, with a moist interior and a frosting that I think I could eat on its own.

Maggie demands the recipe, and she and Val compare notes about their favourite cakes.

I think back to when Rob met Maggie and Tom and how differently they are treating Val. It's as if she has their approval for being part of our family, as crazy as that sounds. I never came to introduce her with the intention of her ever seeing Maggie and Tom again, but she's already arranged to help them with their wills and to share more recipes with my mother.

My parents aren't anti-love. In fact, they're quite the opposite. I've never been in a position to introduce them to anyone before. Perhaps with Tom and Maggie seeing how amazing Val is and how good she'd be for me, Val might be convinced by her family to see the same. When I agreed to be her fake boyfriend, I never thought it would be so hard to get her to notice me as a potential real partner, not just a fictional one.

We take a tour of the garden, taking in the veggie patch that is over-flowing with produce and admiring the apple trees that have tiny fruit on them.

Val has no issues arguing with Tom when he talks about population sustainability and argues for smaller families. Her arguments against his points of view are well thought out and delivered with kindness. It shows the sort of lawyer Val is. She isn't itching for a fight but trying to find ways to make things better and broaden the horizons of others.

Tom nods at Val as we sit again on the verandah and drink tea. "Well, we can agree to disagree, I think. And maybe you're right, the world would be a better place with more people like you populating it, so if you want to have more than two kids with the one partner, then go for it."

"Oh, Tom, I am a one partner girl." Val smiles at my father, who chuckles back. "And I've probably left it too late to have too many kids myself. But one can dream, right?"

I may not be a medical expert, but I know about recessive genes, and I've thought a lot in recent weeks about what any kids Val and I managed to have might look like. She showed me photos of Boyd, Emily, and Issy, and it was fascinating to see her brother with blond hair. She told me one of her other brothers has quite curly hair. I imagine a son with blond curls and a glint in his eye. Maybe a daughter who's a tomboy like her mum.

These thoughts aren't helpful, though, especially when Val has been clear about the fictional nature of our relationship. Harbouring desires for her is not in my best interests. I feel it is too late to stop these feelings though, and I'll just have to put up with the consequences of a broken heart come the end of our weekend at Cassowary Point.

"Rob and I are investigating fostering." Myf's words bring me back to the conversation around me. "So you can have our kids, too, if you want."

There's no sadness behind my sister's statement, and Rob smiles as he rubs her shoulder.

"You're stopping IVF?" Maggie's brow rises.

"We are." Myf nods. "And whilst I think it's a shame Rob's DNA isn't continuing, we're really pleased with our decision."

I knew Myf and Rob had been trying, but I didn't know they'd been doing IVF, something my mother is clearly across. I feel a tinge of sadness for my sister and her husband, even though I know they'll be amazing parents to kids who need it.

"It probably won't lead to adoption, as that's fairly rare these days, but there are some kids needing long-term fostering, and the social worker we've been dealing with thinks Myf and I will be perfect." Rob has his arm around his wife's waist, her head resting on his shoulder.

"That's so exciting." Val clasps Myf's hand, and I have to remind myself that today's the first time they've met, as they're acting like they've known each other for years. I don't think Val realises the effect she has on people and how they naturally respond to her warm and kind nature. It should please me that she's like this, but it's also like a knife to the guts, knowing our arrangement has an expiry date. "If you need me to look over any paperwork, let me know."

"Yeah, her fees are reasonable and cheaper than mine, as she's not a partner." I smirk, and Val shakes her head.

We excuse ourselves and start the trip home when a car appears on the driveway and a couple I vaguely know from my childhood appear. I don't want to think about what they're getting up to with Maggie and Tom as we hit the highway.

It's been a very pleasant afternoon, much nicer than I was expecting. I added little to the conversations, but I sat and listened, taking it all in and getting a better understanding of what makes Maggie and Tom tick. I'd been dreading this trip, worried they'd treat Val poorly, and she'd be begging to leave. In the end, she almost begged to stay before she realised why my parents' friends had probably arrived. Huge hugs were exchanged, with promises that Val would see Maggie and Tom again in a couple of weeks to do their wills. It seems my parents are as infatuated with Val as I am.

# 13

# Val

Despite all Rhys' warnings, I loved meeting Maggie and Tom. Sure, they're a little alternative, but it honestly wouldn't have surprised me if we turned up and they had been naked. Myf is also a delight. Rhys protested, but she sat in the back of the car with me on the way home. We surreptitiously exchanged phone numbers without Rhys knowing, and Myf insisted she drive me to the airport on Thursday.

I've been in court all week. It's one of those annoying cases where the father is represented through Legal Aid and the mother has to extend the mortgage to pay for legal fees. It's a clear-cut case, but the father won't agree to anything and from the get-go has set out to make things challenging.

My client was a rockstar on the stand. She was able to accept her faults leading to the trial, but also emphasise the poor choices her ex had made along the way.

"I never should have married him." She'd sighed as the court adjourned for the day. "I thought I loved him, but I don't think I loved him as much as he loved himself." I hated seeing the worry lines around her face and her sullen, sunken eyes.

"His behaviour this afternoon did not endear himself to the judge, and he'll be back on the stand tomorrow morning to further dig his grave," I reassured her.

My predictions for yesterday had been correct. I could see the judge was as frustrated as I was. When I worked at Legal Aid, I'd been vocal about taking on cases like this where the party was asking for unicorns and fairy dust. As a lawyer, I still believe it's our job to explain to our clients what is fair and reasonable under the law. Sure, sometimes that needs to be stretched a little and tested, but this is not one of those cases.

We almost wrapped things up yesterday, but the judge adjourned early, so we were back this morning for an hour or two. I'd been able to pop into the office to hand over my files to one of the secretaries and then headed home early to pack for my trip up north.

RHYS

How did it go?

It's as if Rhys can tell I've just poured a glass of wine and sat down with my list of things I need to remember for tomorrow.

He has no argument for sole custody. His lawyers could see this, and the fact that our taxpayer dollars are funding him makes me angry.

RHYS

Sounds crappy. So, what did you get me for Valentine's?

I had found the perfect something and hoped Rhys would appreciate it.

It's a surprise! What did you get me?

RHYS

Something…

I should be able to tickle it out of you…

There is a pause in our exchange.

RHYS

> Or else we could just wait and exchange gifts on Saturday.

Party pooper.

RHYS

> Have a safe flight, ok? I'll message you tomorrow night to check things are cool.

They'll be fine. We'll be fine, and I'm sure we will both play our parts perfectly.

I CHECKED off my list as I packed things in my case yesterday, but I do a double-check this morning. There's my dress, shoes, and underwear, as well as my birthday gifts for my siblings and parents. I open the gift bag that contains the gift for Rhys. There's no way he won't appreciate it, and the thought makes me smile.

I've also bought gifts for my nieces. Thinking back to the Christmas when Boyd and Emily gave the kids musical instruments, including a tambourine and maracas, I've found a musical mat that Issy can play with that rings, dings, rattles, and chimes. She's too young for a drum kit, after all.

The cake I baked Dad is sitting on the kitchen bench next to my keys. I need them to lock the door, so I know I won't forget it. My phone is in my hand, and I've packed my charger. Myf should be here any minute. I check the back door is locked and the windows are closed.

My anxiety has ratcheted up, knowing I'll be seeing my family in a few hours and I have to sell Rhys and me as a couple. Part of me says it won't be too hard at all, because we have formed a friendship, but the other part is scared, worried that it will be too convincing, and I'll start to believe that there's something there beyond our acting.

There's a knock at the door. I shake my hands to try to calm my nerves, but I end up dropping my phone.

"You alright?" I hear Myf's muffled voice on the other side of the door.

"Yes," I huff as I swing the door open and pick up my phone. "I'm just a little on edge, you know, having to sell this whole thing to my family and all. Come in."

Myf follows me through to the kitchen where I've left my case. "This place is gorgeous. Did you buy it renovated?"

"No." I chuckle. "I got it for a steal, then spent far too much doing it up. I actually sort of focussed on what I love about my parents' house and scaled it down."

"So, just this suitcase?" Myf wheels my bright-red case towards the door.

"Yep. Thanks." I grab my keys and have to turn back to pick up the cake. I doubt there'll be too much time to bake a replacement cake if I forget this one.

The morning rush has cleared, and the roads are smooth as we make our way to the airport. Myf has hip-hop music playing quietly in the background, her fingers tapping away at the steering wheel to the beat.

"You know he likes you, right?" Myf's head bobs as we stop, waiting for a traffic light to change.

I contemplate ignoring her comment and stare out the window as if I'm really interested in the cars in the secondhand lot on the corner.

"That should make this weekend easier, then. I mean, it would be hard to act like the loving couple if he didn't." My attempt at sarcasm falls a little flat.

"I get the impression you like him, too." Myf stops her tapping, and I look over to see her glancing at me.

"Of course I like him. He's an incredible man. I just can't date anyone I work with. I really don't think I'm built for happily ever afters, and, sure, I'll admit, there's something different about Rhys, but I think it's because it's an act and nothing else."

Myf's eyes go back to the road as the lights change. We listen to the music for a bit as my admission hangs in the air. The truth is, I do like Rhys. He's different from anyone I've been out with before. He's smart, he's respectful, and most of all, he listens. And that's all before I think about his square jaw or the way his glasses give off hot professor vibes. He's the one who's set the expiration date of this thing, though. This isn't really something I want to talk about with his sister, as well meaning as I'm sure she is.

"I dated another midwife for a few months before I met Rob. We split amicably, and I still see her around the hospital," Myf adds after a while. "Maybe you and Rhys both need to have a weekend of hot sex and get it out of your systems, then you can go on being friends."

Myf sees my shoulders shrug as we zoom down the freeway to the airport. So many nights I've dreamt about sex with Rhys. I've actually dreamt of more than sex, of an intimacy I don't think I've known before, one that I've read about in books.

I've dreamt that he holds me and strokes my shoulder, peppering kisses along my collarbone and worshipping me. I've tried to demand what I want from guys in the past, and they've often obliged for a while, but never for long enough. It's more than me being worshipped, though. I've also dreamt of worshipping Rhys, of edging him with the blowjob to end all blowjobs and making him forget the women who have come before me.

Sure, I've had plenty of lovers, and I genuinely love sex. It's my rule that a guy has to give me an orgasm if he wants a second chance, but the reality is, it's not that hard for me to orgasm. I think it's best that I don't discover Rhys' bedroom skills for fear I'll be disappointed either way—he'll be great, and it will be for just a weekend, or he'll be just like all the other guys I've been with, and I'll have to admit I'm never going to find my unicorn.

I can feel heat pooling between my legs and regret forgetting to pack my vibrator. It's not like I can ask Myf to grab one and give it to Rhys to bring up for me. Emily's picking me up, and she'll have Issy, and I don't know if she's ever been into a sex shop, let alone one in Cassowary Point. I may have to make do with my fingers tonight.

Myf pulls up at the kerb to drop me off and gets out to help with my case. She also reminds me to grab the cake which I've almost left on the back seat.

"I'm sure the two of you are going to rock it, and I hope whatever happens, we can keep in touch. I need some friends outside of work, plus Rob and I might need some legal advice if fostering happens."

Myf's hug is firm, and it's easy to return.

"You betcha. I'll text you some photos, and perhaps we can catch up next week?"

"Absolutely." Myf smiles as she releases me, climbs back into her car, and drives away.

EMILY SQUEALS and jumps up and down as she meets me at the airport with baby Issy. I'm amazed by how much she's grown since I saw her in early December. It's almost painful when she clings to her mother and refuses to come to me, even though she's seen me through the screen on our video calls so often.

We make our way to Emily's car, and she straps her daughter in, blowing raspberries on her stomach, making her laugh so hard. It's such a beautiful sound. Emily is a natural mother, and I can't help but wonder how different things could have been for her and Boyd if they hadn't been able to have her.

"You seem calmer. What's going on?" I ask my best friend as we drive to my parents' home.

"I'm having sex again." Emily smiles. "Boyd and I had a great chat after you laid into him. Thank you."

"I just told him the truth, which I think he already knew. He's got it bad for you, woman. He always has had it bad, though." I try not to tease Emily, but I suspect some of my own jealousy shines through.

Regular sex is one thing, but seeing how down pat she has the whole parenting thing is another. I'd be one of those mothers who leaves their child in the shopping cart and drives home without them.

"Yeah, well, I got it bad for him, too. Once he worked out that I wouldn't break, things are, well, they're great again in the bedroom. And the nursery, and the lounge room..." Emily wiggles her eyebrows.

"I get the picture." I laugh. "So, what's planned for the weekend?"

"Hen and Ken have claimed you tonight. Top secret, they told me. All I know is this afternoon, the marquee is being assembled on the lawn, and tomorrow is decoration day. I think Hills and Bridget have the decorations in hand, but I suspect we'll both be needed. What time does your man get in?" Emily indicates the upcoming turn long before she needs to. It amuses me she is the opposite sort of driver to her husband.

"Twenty-four hours after me." I'm distracted as I notice how things have changed in my hometown. An old takeaway shop has turned into a café with lots of potted plants outside. A former Indian restaurant now is branded as Italian, and a medicinal cannabis store has popped up where I think a bank used to be.

"Oh. That's so cute, counting in hours." Emily leans over and squeezes my hand.

I hadn't meant to. My response just came out. I know I need to spin Rhys and my relationship a little with my family before he gets here, but at the same time, I almost miss him. I know he wouldn't step in and try to explain things to people, but he'd stand beside me as we both talked about our relationship. It's easy to say we met at work, because it's true. Perhaps I simply crave having him with me, showing me that the idea of being part of a couple isn't out of my reach, even if it is where he is concerned.

"Are we doing family dinner tomorrow night?" I ask, thinking back to five years ago when Boyd and Emily found out they were pregnant and then that it had been a chemical pregnancy on the same day, the day before the gala ball.

"Charlie's booked a large table at one of the pubs for us all. Hills has arranged hair and makeup for us all on Saturday, and I've arranged mani-pedis." Emily turns into my parents' street, and I see that one house has a new fence and another has had a new paint job. "We start getting ready from mid-morning or something, so I've asked Boyd to look after Rhys for you. Saturday night's Saturday night—the auction is going to be huge. Bigger than ever before. Hills has arranged Sunday brunch for us all, and Boyd and I were hoping to have you and Rhys to dinner Sunday night before you fly out."

"We don't fly out until late on Monday. I had thought of taking Rhys for a drive on Monday to some of the gourmet farms." One of my parents' neighbours is backing their boat into their drive, so we have to wait to get past. Issy babbles quietly in the back, playing with the mobile that hangs over her car seat.

"He likes his food then?" Emily asks.

"Yeah." I bite my lip as I think about Rhys, my voice almost raspy.

"Well, with your cooking, he's bound to be happy." Emily's excitement is infectious. I wonder if she's just happy that Boyd has worked out that he can have sex with her after all, or if she's happy about the gala, seeing the last one was not very memorable for her, or if she really is as happy to see me. Seeing she squealed when she saw me, I'm taking the last option, but I suspect the other two add to her happiness levels.

"Rhys is an amazing cook, too. He loves to fish, and I think he's probably got 101 different fish recipes he can whip up in a jiffy."

"Nice." Emily nods as the boat is reversed up the driveway, and we can finally move. "And is that a cake tin I saw in your hand?"

"Yeah." I laugh. "Dad was complaining I never bake for him. So, what about Bridget and the girls? When do I see them?"

"The girls have been given tomorrow off school to help with the decorations. And they're having hair and makeup done, too. Giles isn't happy about it." Emily laughs, and I wonder what Boyd will be like when Issy is a teenager. "He's not coping with raising daughters. You should hear him complain about how his peers are raising sons. Oh, my gosh. You'd think Giles was a monk before he met Bridget, not the playboy we all know he was."

"It's funny to think of Giles being the father of a teenager. Millie's so much more levelheaded than I was at that age, so he is fortunate." Millie reminds me of Emily with her quiet and studious ways. I was a tomboy, but I was still loud.

"He told me how happy you seemed when he had dinner with you a few weeks back." Emily turns into my parents' drive, and my heart soars when I see the house.

It's home.

I know my parents have bought a unit near Emily's mum and Nonna, but I can't imagine not having this house in our family. It's eclectic, like us. I've experienced so much here, and I'd hate to not be able to come home and visit.

"Did he?" My voice hitches when I see Mum running out to greet us.

"Seems like Rhys might be good for you." Emily shuts off the engine and opens her door.

"Maybe..."

I'm thankful when Henry picks me up to take me to dinner with them. Mum's been asking all sorts of questions about Rhys all afternoon. On the one hand, I'm glad we've spent time getting to know each other and I could answer them all. On the other, it made me realise what a lovely man Rhys is, and I wondered if I would have been able to get to know him better had this excuse not come up.

"Ken's cooked, I hope you don't mind?" Henry taps his hands on the steering wheel as he listens to some sixties boppy number about love. I swear he needs to broaden his musical horizons.

"I love Ken's cooking, you know that. You look excited about something."

It really gladdens my heart seeing Henry so happy. He and Ken are masters at communication now after making such a hash of it at the start of their relationship.

"I have to wait until we're there, I promised him, but, yes, I am very excited. Tell me about this man of yours." Henry dances in his seat. I swear he has ants in his pants.

"Well, Rhys is Boyd's age. He's funny, smart, and articulate, and he makes me laugh. He lives on a boat and, well, he makes me happy." Once again, my bottom lip finds my teeth, and I produce a genuine smile. I'm glad I don't have to lie about Rhys' amazing qualities, even if I am lying about our relationship.

"I can see that. And by that smile, he keeps you happy in the bedroom, too?" Henry flicks my thigh, causing me to jump and both of us to laugh.

"Henry Alexander Dominic Hartman. Shut your mouth. You know I'm a virgin still." I clutch a hand to my chest, enunciating each word as if I'm reading a 1960s news bulletin.

"That ship sailed a long time ago, sis," Henry huffs. "You should know how Emily talks when she has a glass of wine in her. It's even worse now she's had Issy. I know what a hussy you really are."

"I'm going to kill her." I laugh. Our banter is lighthearted.

"Please don't, Boyd would be heartbroken." Henry rolls his eyes. "You'd think he invented love the way he acts around Emily."

Henry pulls up at the new townhouse they recently moved into. It's so much bigger than their old place and suits them.

"Hi, Ken!" I yell as we walk inside their gorgeous home.

"Hey, hon. He didn't tell you, did he?" Ken appears from the kitchen with a glass of wine for me and greets his partner with a kiss.

"No, but he almost peed his pants, holding something in." I sip the wine and let out a moan. Henry and Ken have great taste in food and wine.

They look at each other and giggle. "We're getting married!" They both blurt out together.

"Congratulations," I almost scream as I throw my arms around both of them as they hold each other's faces. "When?"

"Saturday night," Henry says sheepishly, a sly grin on his face.

"And Mum and Dad don't know, do they?" I shake my head, the smile still wide on my face.

"No, and it's a secret and only you know, but, well, our family will be together, and our friends will be there anyway, and we don't need gifts or anything." Henry is prone to blurt things out, and I can now see why he was excited in the car.

"Don't tell me you want a prenup?" I groan.

"Of course not." Ken's brow furrows. "We know your feelings on the subject."

My family is well aware I feel prenuptial agreements are either not worth the paper they're written on, or only drawn up when a couple suspects they won't last. I recognise I'm possibly wrong in my assumptions, but deep down, I believe in the romance of relationships lasting until your partner dies.

Henry ushers us into their lounge area, and I take a seat on their gorgeous white sectional couch.

"You see, hon"—I've always loved the way Ken calls me hon, knowing I'm the only member of my family to receive this privilege—"we've got a friend who has two spawns of her own and doesn't want any more, but she did great at being pregnant and all..."

"You've found a surrogate?" I ask, almost tipping over my wine glass as I lean over to grab Henry's hand.

"We have, but legally?" He frowns, his top lip meeting his teeth.

I explain the legal options where we live as far as I'm aware and tell them I would research more when I get back to the office. I'm so thrilled for my brother and his partner. I know Mum will scream when they stand up to be married, and Dad will be happy for them. My other brothers will probably shake their heads and wish the happy couple well.

The idea of more children possibly joining our family is exciting, but it also makes me feel so far away in Brisbane.

"The other thing." Henry holds Ken's hand, and I can see him squeeze it gently. "Will you be our best woman? Christian has agreed to be our best man, but you're my baby sister, and we don't see you enough, and I want you to be part of our day."

Christian has been Henry's best friend for years. He's also become close to Ken. When he left school, Christian studied engineering, but he decided after a few years he hated it and went back to study medicine. He now works at Cassowary Point Hospital and is training to be an orthopaedic surgeon.

I had a huge crush on Christian when I was a teenager, even though he's seven years older than me. Every time I've seen him over the last couple of years at one of our extended family gatherings, though, he's been gazing longingly at Ken's sister, Dipti, and I often wonder what's going on there.

With tears streaming down my face, I nod, and my voice cracks as I say, "Yes." Despite the mix-ups I helped create at the start of their relationship, there's been no lasting animosity thrown my way. I'm close to all my brothers, but Henry and I have always shared a close bond.

"I told Giles he was my favourite brother, but I think he just lost the privilege." I laugh through my tears. They truly are tears of joy.

Dinner is lovely, and I notice Henry and Ken smiling at each other when Rhys and I text back and forth throughout the night.

"Emily said your dress is gorgeous, and I think I trust her judgement..." Henry takes a sip of wine before topping up our glasses.

I show him a photo of the dress, and he clutches his hands to his chest and tells me it's perfect. "Rhys is a lucky man to be stepping out with you in it."

As I lie in my old bed that night, sleep eludes me. I haven't come up with a story as to how Rhys and I will break up. Several possibilities run through my head. I can't lay the blame at his feet, because he's being so good about the entire arrangement. My family knows I'm choosy, and I suspected I will have to, in the end, tell them Rhys could not put up with my idiosyncrasies or tell them we weren't well suited in the bedroom.

I toss and turn, wondering what it's like to sleep on *Serenity*. I had a glance at Rhys' cabin when he showed me around the boat on my first outing on her. It's not the sleeping on a boat I'm intrigued about, though—it's sleeping with Rhys. I've been so vocal about my rules about orgasms with partners that telling people Rhys and I aren't well suited sexually seems a little odd.

It's not like I've explored a lot of kink; I'm not entirely vanilla, but I wouldn't say I was rocky road either. I like a swirl of something through my vanilla, enough to overpower it sometimes, but not enough that I can't get a spoonful of the plain flavour when I want it.

Rhys doesn't strike me as having kinks that I would find too out there. I mean, he accepts his parents and their lifestyle, but has told me it's not for him. He didn't bat an eyelid when Myf was explaining herself as being a disaster bisexual, simply laughing that he was the only straight one in their family.

Sleep must come eventually, because I dream about Rhys stroking his hands down my back in the red gown I'm wearing for the gala, except we're dancing on the deck of *Serenity*. He's whispering into my ear that we're sailing into the sunset together and that everything will work out fine. I wake as the waters are getting choppy and hope that the weekend with Rhys will be smooth sailing and not a cataclysmic storm.

I risk so much in lying to my family. The sincerity Henry and Ken showed last night thinking that I'd finally found my one made me almost regret the lie. I know part of it is fear. I'm scared of being swept up in the fairy tale, but I need to remind myself that the situation with Rhys is fake. We're playing roles that we wouldn't play in real life, and that's why spending time with him feels so perfect.

My family are the only ones who can accept me for being me. They joke about my forgetfulness, and Giles still ribs me about not being a doctor, but their love is unconditional. I hope it remains that way when they either find out about my deception of not being in a relationship with Rhys to begin with or when Rhys and I 'break up.'

It's still early, but I can hear people outside setting up for the gala. No doubt we'll all be called upon to help string up fairy lights and turn the space into a wonderland. It still amazes me that Mum pulls this off every five years.

I make my bed, conscious that Rhys will be seeing my room today. I suspect he'll be in Boyd's room, so I'll have to double-check it's presentable. My room is all teenage Val. It has pale-grey walls and book-cases filled with novels. The window overlooks the pool, the place Boyd and Emily married each other all those years ago. I love that Henry and Ken are going to surprise everyone with their wedding, too.

Skipping down the stairs towards the kitchen, I can hear Mum humming a song that I'm sure she's heard from Henry's love song playlist.

She greets me with a kiss on my cheek. "You look tired, sweetheart. Not sleeping well without your man next to you? I never sleep well when your father's not around."

"Gee, thanks, Mum." I roll my eyes. "It's just strange being back home again. I forgot about how much I do like it up here and how nice it is being close to my brothers and their partners."

Mum pours me a cup of tea. I'm not at all surprised she has a fresh one at hand. "Do you think Rhys would move up here?"

I know he's lived here before, and he's told me he likes the area. It's hard selling our supposed love story when I'm so torn about it all. On one hand, Rhys is amazing, the sort of guy I can imagine being with in the future. On the other, my career is important to me, and I want to work with my colleagues not having to pick sides when we eventually break up, because as history shows, guys always break up with me.

"I'm not sure. We've not talked about it." I sip my tea and marvel at how my parents' brew always tastes different to the tea I make myself.

"Well, no doubt he'll fall in love with the place as much as he's fallen in love with you." Mum has cut up some fruit and almost moans as she takes a bite of the pineapple. I lean over for a piece and can see why; the sweetness is just right.

"Mum, you haven't met him yet. It's too early for you to be talking about love. Which room do you want him in tonight, by the way?"

Mum looks at me with a raised eyebrow. "Why yours, of course. It would be cruel to separate lovebirds over Valentine's." She crosses her arms and leans against the bench. "Don't look so shocked. Your father and I both realise you two are sleeping together. Even your father's not that old-fashioned as to believe you're still a virgin. What was it, young Michael Nielsen after that pool party?"

"Mother!" I shriek, my brain going back to sixteen-year-old me giving in to the guy who'd followed me around like a lovesick puppy for years.

"Whatever happened to him?" Mum pours the tea leaves into the container that she stores them in before taking them out and sprinkling them around the garden.

"Last I heard, he was in sales working down south and happily married with a gaggle of children." I shrug. It's not like we've kept in touch. Michael was a nice boy, but he never was right for me.

"It could have been you, you know." Mum raises her eyebrows and looks to the heavens.

"Mother. Really?" I sigh. "I was never like Emily and was not going to settle as a teen."

"Well, get a move on, will you—we still haven't got a grandson."

"Thanks, Mum, I'll keep it in mind," I say sarcastically.

I know she means well, but she just reminds me why I can't move back here as a single woman. I need to come back partnered or not at all.

# 14

# Rhys

ALL WEEK, MYF'S BEEN BLOWING UP MY PHONE WITH PLANS on how I can convince Val we're perfect together. I know she wants to see me happy, but her plans are bordering on insane. No, I'm not going to steal Val away on *Serenity* and refuse to return to shore until she's agreed to be my girlfriend. Neither am I going to propose to her in front of everyone at the gala ball.

Myf's met a few of my girlfriends in the past, but she's never been this enthusiastic. I'm hanging on by a thread in my mind, recognising this is an arrangement, a role to play until the weekend is over. All I can hope is the weekend is a huge success, and we pretend to go our own ways from the airport on Monday evening, only for me to pester Val into joining me on *Serenity*, or for a coffee, or for any chance of spending time together.

I'll be able to remind her how well we worked together, and we can build something from there. Maybe I'll be able to break down her defences, and she'll finally see how great we could be together.

MYF

> Dinner. Tonight. Not taking no for an answer.
> Also, I'm taking you to the airport tomorrow.

I've got a lift already tomorrow.

I don't, but I can easily catch a cab.

MYF

Dinner then. Don't make me send Rob to drag you here. I'm cooking pasta, the homemade stuff.

Damn my sister. She knows I'm a sucker for her homemade pasta. She's already told me she has today and tomorrow off, and I know Dad gave her some of his homemade cheese last weekend.

I head into the office, knowing Val is already on her way to Cassowary Point. I haven't seen her since our trip to see my parents. Part of me was concerned Val would run a mile once she met Maggie and Tom, but they were on their best behaviour, and Val charmed them. She and Maggie talked cakes for half the afternoon before Val took photos of some of Mum's favourite cake recipes, handwritten recipes given to her by friends over the years. Maggie was prepared to write them out for her, but Val explained it was easier to snap a photo. At one stage, I thought she'd convinced Maggie it was time to get a mobile phone, but even Val couldn't convince her of that.

Tom loved that Val took an interest in the garden and was keen to hear about the native Australian produce he was growing. When Val and Maggie poured over recipes, Tom took the time to tell me that he thought Val was one of the decent lawyers out there. Sure, he went all hippie on me and tried to tell me she's the yin to my yang, and then he developed a sardonic smile on his face when I tried to remind him Val and I are involved in an arrangement to get her family off her back.

Thank heavens their friends pulled up just as Maggie was pulling out her tarot cards. She'd already examined Val's palm with interest, telling Val there were plenty of children in her future and a long love line, whatever that means. I had to laugh when she was kissing me good-bye, and she whispered in my ear that Val would have a baby by the end of the year. That would involve sex, and there's been none of that. I've never believed in Maggie's fortune telling and think that most of the time it's either lucky guesses or predictions that are so vague, they're bound to be a possibility.

Having a baby by the end of the year is not one of those, though. The children in her future are probably her nieces. There'll be no point telling Maggie how wrong she is when the time comes. Naturally, I don't want her to be wrong. I don't know how I've gone from lusting after this woman from afar to thinking a baby before Christmas would be amazing.

"Hey, mate." Rob is in my office before I've put my briefcase down and taken a seat. "All packed?"

"I collected my suit from the dry cleaner on the way here, but otherwise, I'm set. What have you got for me?" I push my glasses up my nose as I wait for Rob to open the folder he's holding.

"Don't forget condoms." Rob chuckles. "If it's not on, it's not on."

I glare at him with a flat mouth, my teeth grinding together. Rob gets the message and slides some papers across to me, coloured tabs stuck where I need to sign. I almost tear a hole in the paper with my pen as I jerk the nib across the page, pressing far too hard.

At least Rob is quiet as I sign. I should never have told him early on that I think Val is amazing. After I finish leaving my mark on what feels like a dozen documents, I hand them back. I'm a little less tense, but I don't want Rob to think he can carry on his goading of me.

"I'll be at yours around six, okay? It won't be a late night for me though." I put the lid on my pen and put it in my drawer without looking up at him.

I'm angry with myself for agreeing to this setup, really. Spending four days with Val is going to be tortuous. I mean, it will be amazing, but the torture will be knowing that our arrangement is coming to an end.

There's a box hiding in my in-tray along with a couple of law journals. I haven't ordered anything recently, and I never get things delivered to the office, so I open it tentatively. A packing slip is enclosed with a message that simply says, 'Thanks for being the best fake boyfriend ever. Here's to a great weekend. Val. PS- this isn't your Valentine's gift, just a thank you for being your amazing self.'

Inside the box is a Kindle, the same model as Val's. My heart swells, and before my brain catches up, I try to read into this generous gesture. But the card is clear. I'm her fake boyfriend, no matter what my heart might want. I reach for my phone to send Val a message.

> Santa came late to my office and delivered a Kindle. Thanks. Being a fake boyfriend is no hardship at all.

As soon as I send the message, I wonder if I've said the right thing. I mean, it's the truth, as hard as it is to say. The hardship is knowing she sees it as fake and not the truth I'd like it to be.

VAL

> You are more than welcome. I'm glad you called at the office before you flew out. I was worried and didn't want to give Rob any more ammunition, as he seems to forget that this is just an arrangement.

> Tell me about it.

VAL

> I'm just with Mum and Emily, but I'll text later. I'll also email you a list of books I think you should download. It came with some vouchers, too, which I'll send through so you can start your library. Oh, and Mum and Emily say hi. Apparently, ignoring them to answer your texts is seen as being romantic. Insert eye roll.

> Well, thanks again. It's a lovely surprise.

"BROTHER!" Myf shrieks as she opens the door and throws her hands above her head as if she's about to break into a song and dance.

"Here as demanded." I'm embraced in a hug, which melts a little of the frosty disposition that has followed me around all afternoon.

"Come through, come through." Myf drags me to the kitchen where Rob is chopping herbs.

I need to apologise for snapping at him earlier, but Myf gets in first. "All packed? Got the silk boxer shorts and plenty of condoms?"

"Don't go there." Rob shakes his head as he drops the knife on the chopping board.

"No, it's okay." I sigh. "Get it out of your systems now, and then we can enjoy dinner."

"Have you at least shaved your balls? No one enjoys getting hair between their teeth when they're massaging your balls with their tongue."

"I'll take that under advisement," I deadpan.

I've never shaved my balls, and I'm not about to start now. I won't dictate what my partner does with her pubic hair, and I don't expect anyone to dictate the same to me. Except, I can't help but wonder if Val might prefer me smooth down there. Shit. I can't believe I'm actually using brain cells to worry about stuff like this.

"Are you sure you're sorted for a lift tomorrow?" Myf drops ravioli into boiling water as Rob passes me a glass of wine.

"Yep," I say, my voice still sounding irritated. "Look"—I rub my hand over my face, dislodging my glasses—"I know you both mean well, but this really is an act this weekend to get Val's parents off her back. Come Monday, we're back to being colleagues, and we forget this ever happened."

"Except you like her, like her." Myf sounds like she's a teenager.

"Val is a gorgeous, accomplished woman. But she's said time and time again that she won't date anyone she works with. I've just made partner, and I'm not about to move firms because of a woman."

"Yeah, but it's not like you're in the office all the time. And you work in totally different areas of the law." Rob points his bottle of beer at me.

"But we work at the same firm, and we're small, and I can see where she's coming from." I catch a drop of condensation that threatens to slide down my glass.

"Well, I think she likes you." Myf transfers the parcels of pasta to the sauce where they sizzle in the buttery goodness.

"And I like her, too, but I also need to respect her boundaries and decisions."

We sit around the kitchen bench to eat. Myf is an excellent cook, and this pasta is exceptional. I mull over her words, though, as she and Rob prattle on about this and that. I respect women. Heck, I respect people. In my head, I can't see any way in which Val would change her mind about dating a colleague. She told me there were colleagues who had a messy breakup at her first job, and I have to wonder if she was one of the said colleagues.

I want to plan for ways to make our weekend together unforgettable, but without coming on too strong. Even then, though, I doubt I'll be able to get Val to change her mind. She's so set in her determination not to date someone from work. There's no way I'll be the one to break that.

VAL

> OMG you're never going to guess this one.

You've been introduced to a doctor colleague of someone in your family, and they're the one?

Even though I love that Val is texting me during dinner with my sister- and brother-in-law, my fear is she will meet someone else this weekend.

VAL

> Er, no, plus I wouldn't do that to you. Hen and Ken are getting married at the gala, but it's top secret. I'm one of a handful of people to know, and I'm going to be their best woman. You can't tell anyone, but I needed to share with someone. So excited for them!

That's great news.

Jesus. I mean, sure, it is good news, but I could have been a little more enthusiastic.

"Who are you texting?" Myf leans over my shoulder, and I clasp my phone to my chest.

"None of your business." I know I sound defensive, which only makes my sister smile.

"Say hi to Val from me." Myf squeezes my shoulder as she takes away my plate.

I stand to help with the dishes, and my phone vibrates again.

> **VAL**
>
> It's lovely being back with them, and you seem to be a great buffer. There's been no talk of doctors or setting me up with anyone.

> Maybe it's because you look genuinely happy.

> **VAL**
>
> Yeah, well, I've got the equivalent of blue balls, and I forgot to pack a vibrator. If I climb you when I see you, it's just my natural urges taking over, okay? Think a judge and jury would buy that?

Rob's thrown a tea towel at me, and I'm drying a glass bowl. Foolishly, I left my phone screen side up on the bench, and I don't want Myf or Rob to see it. I try to stand in front of it, but Myf needs to get to the drawer. I slide my phone down the bench with my elbow, which causes Myf to raise an eyebrow. She goes to open the drawer to put away the cutlery, but sweeps around me at the last minute and dives for my phone, just as I connect to it with my arm.

It goes flying, and it feels like everything is in slow motion as I see it head for the tiled floor.

"Children." Rob shakes the suds from his hands and reaches to grab a towel to dry them.

I reach down to grab it, grateful it's in one piece, the case and screen protector doing their job.

> Sorry, my phone went flying. I honestly don't know how to respond to that in a way that doesn't make me sound like a creep.

VAL

LOL. It's all good. Sorry I made you toss your phone across the deck. Lucky it didn't go overboard.

I'm at Myf and Rob's—dragged here for dinner.

VAL

Say hi to them from me.

Will do. Talk tomorrow.

*Talk about mixed signals.*

I CAN'T BELIEVE it's happened. At last, I'm here in Val's childhood bedroom with my head between her legs. I'm trying to get out of my head how much this room looks like Myf's did growing up. I always thought Val would taste like ambrosia, but it's even better than that. After our make out session, she finally grabbed my shirt and slid it over my head. The look of lust in her eyes as she stroked her fingers down my chest almost saw me come on the spot. Trying to control myself, I've tossed her back on the bed, and my tongue is exploring her.

She's so responsive. Her hands tug at my hair as she pulls me closer, moaning for more. She seems to love when I create a seal around her clit and suck whilst flicking the tip of my tongue over it. Her juices flow when I stick my tongue deep inside her, my tongue wishing it was my cock.

I'm not prepared for her to detonate like she does, her back arching, bottom lifting off the bed, and her chanting my name over and over. I don't think there's ever been a sweeter song from her lips.

We've waited weeks for this—or even months, in my case really—and it's better than I could ever have imagined.

Suddenly, my condom-clad cock is notching at her entrance as she tries to pull me inside her. Our lips meet, and she licks her juices off them as if she wants to devour me.

"Please, just fuck me. I've wanted this for so long but been so scared. I need you, Rhys." Her voice is more than sultry; it's allure and temptation rolled into one.

I can feel her walls stretch to accommodate me and hear the little whimpers leave her mouth as she wraps her legs around my hips, trying to draw me deeper. Never have I felt this close to a woman in my life. I want to tell her I'm in love with her and want to spend my life with her. I want to make babies with her and encourage her in whatever dreams she has.

As I rock my hips, I feel our pubic bones press together. I thrust a little, slowly at first, but I can see Val wants more. Her legs are strong, drawing me into her as our lips and tongues duel for dominance. Val's hands explore my back, neck, and head, as if they can't decide where they want to touch most.

I do not know who initiates the change in position, but soon, I'm on my back, Val enveloping me with her gorgeous pussy as she rides me. Her breasts respond to the touch of my fingers, then my tongue, as I drag her down on me. I need to think of something to stop me from blowing too soon. I want this to go on forever.

The sounds Val makes fill my ears, urging me to delay my gratification to eke out a second orgasm from her. Too soon, she's spasming around my cock, but her voice is strange, a robotic chime that sounds awfully like my alarm.

I can't decide if I'm more embarrassed or disgusted with myself when I realise it was a dream and I wake up in a pool of my own cum. Fuck, I need to clean up. I don't have time to wash my sheets, as I'm meeting with a client before heading to the airport. We're doing breakfast at a local café.

My mind isn't on legal matters and the sale of the yacht he purchased only a few months ago. It's on Val and what the weekend will bring for us. I've told her I'll play the part of a doting boyfriend. Except, it's not a part. It's a role I've been desiring for months. I'm going to have to ensure I can spend a weekend playing what she thinks is a part and come away with my heart intact. It sounds like an impossible task, but I know I'll get through this weekend and come back to lick my wounds. I'll respect Val and her wishes, even if her wishes don't align with mine.

"So, what's this slight change in plans?" I greet Val at Cassowary Point airport with an enormous hug. She left a message that had been waiting for me as I waited to disembark the plane.

At first, I was worried that the game was up, and I'd simply be jumping on a return flight to Brisbane—my services no longer needed. The hug Val gave me was reassuring, though. We'd only shared a couple of hugs, and they were amazing. The way our bodies fit together like they were designed to possibly led to my dream this morning. She plays with her hands as we separate from the hug.

"Mum is suddenly all enlightened and doesn't want to separate us, so she can't see why we wouldn't share a room this weekend." Val bites her bottom lip between her teeth.

"I see." My heart races, but I keep my voice steady. Three nights sharing a bed with Valerie Hartman could be the undoing of me.

"I mean, it's a double bed, so it's not that big, and there's a chaise on one side of the wall, so I could sleep there." Val looks at me with tears in her eyes. Does she not realise that this is no hardship for me?

"I'm not kicking you out of your bed," I promise as I reach for her hand. "We'll work something out."

She doesn't complain as we make our way to the car, our fingers entwined. It feels so natural and so right.

"I mean, I shouldn't be surprised. Boyd and Emily lived together at Mum and Dad's when they were at uni," Val sighs. "Now, it's hush-hush about Henry and Ken, remember?"

I climb into the car, a very nice Audi that Val says was a gift from her father to her mother last year.

"Of course. Is there anything else I'm meant to know or not know?" I'm staring out the window, captivated by the lushness of the place.

Val knows her way around the streets of Cassowary Point. I spent more time on the water and down by the marina than in the suburbs when I lived here, clearly missing out on a lot the place has to offer. We drive down streets with large tropical trees lining them and past the botanic gardens.

"I don't think so. Bridget and the girls and Emily and Mum are decorating the marquee. They'll probably love your help stringing fairy lights or something." Val sounds excited and smiles when she glances at me as we stop at a traffic light.

"I can do that, no problems." I smile back. "How long have they been holding these galas?"

"The first one was for their silver anniversary. It was at that gala that Giles proposed to Bridget."

"That's sweet." Val drives up a street in an elevated part of town and pulls up outside a stunning two story home with a large wraparound porch. It's on a decent-sized block, large enough for a sizeable marquee to have been erected to the side of it. "Wow." My eyes bulge, and I lean forward to stare out the car window. "Is this your parents' home?"

"Yep. They bought the old house as newlyweds and extended it. I'll give you the tour," Val says as we climb out of the car, a beep sounding to show she has locked it with the fob in her hand.

"I'm surprised Mum hasn't come running to meet you, but I suspect she's distracted by the decorations. Dad's sensible and is at work."

Val walks me into the home she grew up in. I leave my bags by the staircase that leads to the bedrooms, and she once again takes my hand. She points out the cupboard under the stairs where she used to hide from her brothers and read in, and the bookcases in the den that her father tries to pretend is a study, but her mother has a chair in with her craft supplies next to it. It's truly a stunning home.

"I think they still escape in here most nights; it's got a stunning breeze that flows through these windows."

"So, this is part of the extension?" I ask, trying to ascertain what is the original and what has been tacked on.

"Yep. Well, half of it is. Part of this used to be a small bedroom, apparently. The dining room is new, and the kitchen was extended. The guest room is the old main bedroom. Upstairs there were two poky little rooms, and they were able to totally redo it. It was finished just before Boyd was born. Giles remembers part of it, and there are lots of photos I'm sure they'd love to show you."

I can see why Val loves this place so much. The staircase is wide enough for us to walk side by side, Val carrying my suit carrier in one hand, and me, my larger bag. We place them in her bedroom, which looks nothing like the room I dreamt I was in last night. I can't work out if this is a good thing or not.

There's no time to explore Val's room further before she drags me down the hallway to another bedroom. "And this is Mum and Dad's room. It should be presentable." Val opens the door and pokes her head in before slinging it wide and ushering me in. "They had the bed custom-built and always encouraged my brothers and me to join them in it when we were growing up. I can never remember Giles in there now because he was always that much older than me, but it is a place of comfort to me. And this is their ensuite, complete with the most stunning bath."

"It's beautiful," I almost whisper. There's an amazing view from one window towards the hills that surround Cassowary Point. Everything's so white, fresh, and, well, homely. "It feels like it's got love seeping out of every crevice. It's hard to describe."

"Yeah. It's funny"—Val smiles—"for all the focus on Valentine's Day, this place oozes love, and I suppose love has always been the focus of the family, not just on one day of the year. Mum and Dad have bought an apartment in the same complex Emily's mum and Nonna moved into, and they are threatening to sell this place. I can't see them leaving here, though."

"Even though it's just the two of them?" I ask, again drawn to the view of the hills from the window.

"The grandkids are often over," Val says as we leave their room and make our way back downstairs. "The pool's through here."

My breath hitches as I take in the ocean view. I can't believe whoever first built this house didn't think of capturing this view from the windows. "Now, that is gorgeous. Look at the water. It stretches for miles. I can only imagine how amazing the sunrise is from up here."

"You passed Dad's test—I'll have to tell him."

"Tell who?" a booming voice comes from behind us.

"Dad! I didn't know you were home. Happy Birthday." Val drops my hand and throws her arms around her father's neck, planting a kiss on his cheek. He squeezes her tight. Pulling away, she again comes to my side and takes my hand. "Dad, this is my partner, Rhys Evans. Rhys, this is my father, Charles Hartman."

"It's Charlie, and I'm so glad to meet the man who finally has made my daughter happy." Val has her father's eyes, and they dance with delight as his lips curl up in a massive smile.

"She's an easy one to please. I mean, a shoulder rub and a book, and she's content." I look at Val, wondering if she notices the love in my eyes.

"I'm so glad you've found a keeper, darling." Charlie casts his eyes between us, and I swear he blinks back a tear.

"Thanks, Dad," Val says as I drape my arm over her shoulder and draw her to my side, where she melts into me.

Just as I thought, it's not a challenge to try to pull this off.

"Now, darling, why don't you go back to helping your mother, and I'll take Rhys on the rest of the tour? I gather he passed the view test?" Charlie pats me on the shoulder, but there's no sign of this being a test. There are no threats or fear he's going to lecture me.

"He did, Dad, with flying colours." I drop a kiss to Val's head, and she lets go of my hand. Being this close to her feels so natural. I'm not sure how Val can't see this isn't an act.

15

# Val

I HAD NOT PREDICTED FEELING THE EXCITEMENT I DID WHEN collecting Rhys at the airport and preparing to show him off to my family. Hours later, I can still feel his hug as his arms wrapped around me and held me close. I had also not thought about how my family would like Rhys. I mean, I should have expected it with his easygoing attitude and droll personality, but he fit right into our family dynamic.

"Now you have to go around and identify everyone," Mum jokes as she places her hands on Rhys's shoulders at the pub. Rhys can easily name everyone, which makes them all laugh. It was the extra titbits of information though that endeared him to everyone, not just me.

"Bridget, never to be called Bridge, because she isn't a structure that crosses water. Ken, who I have to thank for giving Val the best fish curry recipe. I was so glad when she brought me leftovers for my work lunch last week." I'm glad he doesn't add that I didn't take any for myself, knowing colleagues would raise eyebrows. "Boyd with the rooster, not to be confused with the dog of the same name, Mia, who plays the piano as well as, if not better, than her Aunt Emily."

Rhys continues around the table, and my heart swells with the little anecdotes he attaches to the members of my family. "She's coached you well, Rhys." Mum taps his shoulders and plants a kiss on his head.

"Val speaks so highly of her family that it was almost as if I knew you all before I met you." Rhys looks around the table at everyone, still gripping my hand in his lap. I wasn't sure if people could see it, but I knew it was there, and we were in this together, a united front against my family.

Except I wasn't against my family. I realised in being with them that I adore them all and miss them terribly. I feel awful for deceiving them like this, pretending to be in a relationship when I've made my stance clear.

"We miss our Valerie." Mum moves her hands to wrap around my neck. "But it's so nice to find she's met someone as delightful as you, dear Rhys. Now, have you ever considered medicine?"

I groan as Mum heads back to her seat next to Dad.

Rhys gets on well with all my family, chatting to Millie about her upcoming debate audition at school. I know she'll be a shoo-in. He listened when Giles explained the new cardiac stents he was co-designing and so proud of, as if they were the most interesting thing he'd ever heard about. *They aren't, trust me.* What struck me though was when he was busy in conversation with Boyd, I saw Giles smile and wink at me from the other side of the table.

"Is Giles drunk?" I ask Emily. "He keeps winking at me."

"He can see how happy you are and is as thrilled as the rest of us." Emily is trying to get Issy to eat mashed vegetables, but she wants none of it, reaching out for a fry on her mother's plate.

"It's early days still. I mean, I don't have the best track record when it comes to relationships. This one might fizzle out like the rest of them." I shrug.

Seeing Rhys fit in so well and knowing him so much better after spending this time with him, I admit, I'm questioning why I've kept him at arm's length. He spent hours with my dad this afternoon sitting by the pool just talking. He said they talked about *Serenity* and life on the water. I loved that he never flinched when Mum gave him the third degree after we finally finished in the marquee.

"I doubt it." Emily relents and passes Issy a fry, which she gladly gums. "Blind Freddy can see how much Rhys adores you. I assume he goes alright where it matters?"

"Emily," I hiss. "Issy can hear."

"I'll take that as a yes, because if it wasn't, you would have dumped him by now. She's also heard much worse from her father telling her to get to sleep so he can fuck me. And again, I know I've got you to thank for that."

If I'd been up here, I would have seen sooner that there was a strain on my brother and best friend's marriage. I still don't know who Boyd talked to, but they had clearly resolved their issues.

"More than welcome, and hey, maybe he is a dud, and I'm only keeping him around to stop all of you from marrying me off to a doctor."

"Yeah right. You know what those long fingers mean." Emily scoffs, digging into my ribs with her elbow. "I mean, they look almost longer than Boyd's."

"Emily. Please." I shake my head as the words come out of my mouth as a groan.

"What is my wife going on about now?" Boyd asks, turning to Emily and kissing her hand.

"Just penises, my love," Emily replies, causing me to drop my head to the table and wish the ground would open.

"You have a theory, Emily? Is this a medical fact?" I'm surprised to see Rhys entering the conversation.

"In my clinical studies, long fingers can be a very good indicator of the length of other appendages, yes." Emily gazes at her husband, who kisses her head and mumbles something in her ear that makes her laugh.

"Boyd, Rhys, put your palms together," Emily instructs the men, reaching across both of us and following her demands. "Wow, Rhys, your fingers are longer than Boyd's. Girl, you must be singing from the hilltops." Emily fans herself as she turns to me with a wink.

"Well, she hasn't complained yet..." I look at Rhys as he also winks at me, and I can't help but smile and laugh.

I don't need to be thinking about the size of Rhys's cock when I've made my position on workplace relationships clear. My first week at Legal Aid, I went out for a drink with Tanner, who seemed like a nice guy. He was charming, but there was something about him that made me not actually head back to his place and sleep with him. I couldn't have cared if he was a colleague or not, but I just wasn't feeling it, whatever it was.

He then went out with another woman in the office for a month or so, and when that soured, things were horrible. She was amazing about it all, but Tanner tried to ruin her career and told lies about her, inventing a fake cocaine addiction and trying to get her disbarred.

Rhys is nothing like Tanner. As a lawyer, I need to read people, and Rhys doesn't send up any red flags. He's always respected my boundaries and never complained, even though I wonder at times if he's doing this not only to help me out.

I talked with Janet when I got back to the office on Wednesday and updated her on how I felt Rhys and I were prepared for the weekend. She tried to convince me that perhaps I should give things with Rhys a go, except I can't decide if he is just trying to help me because he likes me, or if that's the sort of person he is.

When I first met him, I thought Rhys was so shy, but now he must feel comfortable with me and my family, because tonight, he's bantered with the best of them, and I know how much my siblings and their partners can throw lines back and forth.

Rhys fits in, and this scares me. Part of me hopes that this might be more than an act and there may be some sort of future for us both.

"I HOPE I didn't overstep the mark earlier with Emily and fingers and stuff..."

Rhys and I have made our way to my room after a lovely cup of tea with my parents when we returned from the pub. Dad even wiped away a tear when I produced the cake I baked for him. He's such a softie, and I love him for it. Because of him, I've never questioned men showing emotions.

"Not at all." I shake my head and want to reach up and stroke his cheek with my hand, but I refrain. "I think you handled it perfectly, and I was not surprised." Again, we left downstairs holding hands.

It's been a common thing today and feels so right. Just as with our hugs, our hands fit perfectly together, too. We haven't been overly affectionate towards each other, just the hand holding and gentle touches here and there. It's not something we practiced, but it hasn't needed practice, as it has just comes so naturally to both of us.

"How are we going to manage tonight?" Rhys asks as I close the door to my room.

"Look, I think it's only sensible that we both try to sleep, and a bed is best for that. I'll take one side, and you can take the other." I make my way to the side of the bed, away from the door, unable to look at Rhys. In my mind, I can't work out if this is a good idea or not, and I don't want his facial expressions to sway me away from us sharing a bed. "Now, I will warn you, I usually sleep naked, and even though I'll wear a T-shirt to bed, I have been known to take it off in my sleep."

"That could be interesting." I look and see Rhys swallow, his Adam's apple bobbing.

"Don't get any ideas, mister, unless, well, I mean..." My voice starts out playful, but softens towards the end of the sentence.

"I think that would definitely complicate things," Rhys says as he comes around the bed and draws me in for another of his wonderful hugs. "Is it okay with you if I just wear my jocks to bed? I'm like you and usually sleep naked, too."

"Fine by me. I mean, I've felt your back putting on sunscreen, and I know where you're ticklish, anyway." I try to regulate my voice, but it comes out higher than usual.

I wonder if Rhys can feel my heart beating much quicker than usual through our hug.

"Don't start what you don't plan to finish." Rhys pulls away, and I have to blink to break the intense eye contact. It's enough for my heart to race and wetness to pool between my thighs.

I head to the bathroom to brush my teeth and apply my face cream, and I smile at the thought of sleeping with a man platonically. I could not remember ever having a man in my bed and not being physical with him. Do I want to be intimate with Rhys, though? I do, but I try not to let myself think about him this way.

"Bathroom's all yours," I say as I walk back into my room to find Rhys studying my bookshelves.

As he uses the bathroom, I slip off my shorts and bra and climb into the far side of the bed. I don't even have any pyjamas here. My T-shirt meets my undies, but doesn't even cover my bum. I need to make sure I'm in bed with the sheet up before Rhys gets back.

I've never had a man in bed with me at my parent's place. Yeah, I'd snuck into the pool shed with lovers occasionally but never actually had sex in my childhood room. I figured I'd face away from the door, and that way, Rhys could come and climb into bed when he returned, and I would not have to look at him in his undies. What I didn't see and know about, I couldn't miss.

Rhys returns and shuts the door. I can hear him undressing, and my heart races again.

"You don't want to read for a bit?" Rhys asks as he climbs in next to me.

"I usually do, to get myself sleepy, and I've almost finished this novel I'm reading..." I turn onto my back and catch a glimpse of Rhys in his black boxer briefs. I almost wish I hadn't seen what I was missing out on. The outline alone showed me I was missing out on a lot.

"Go on, grab it. I want to read, too." Rhys has his new eReader in his hand.

I blink as I realise Rhys is talking about my book, not the thing in his shorts I wouldn't mind grabbing. I reach for the book I had placed on the bedside table and sit up next to him in the bed to read.

There's a knock at the door. "Are you two decent?"

"Mother!" I shout as she opens the lockless door and pokes her head in.

"Don't you just look the perfect couple? I just wanted to let you know I put extra towels in your bathroom, that's all." Mum has a giant smile on her face, the hand not on the door handle pressed against her chest.

"Thanks, Hills. Goodnight." Rhys looks over and smiles at her, and she shuts the door.

"Goodnight, lovers!" she yells through the door as she makes her way back to her room, no doubt to tell Dad all about how cozy we look in bed together.

"I'm sorry about her," I say, my book in my lap as I rub my eyes.

"I like her," Rhys reassures me as he squeezes my thigh.

"Dad cornered me at dinner and told me how perfect you are. You must have made an impression on him this afternoon." I pick up my book, finding my place in the last chapter.

"I'm not perfect." Rhys chuckles.

"You'll do." I bump my shoulder against his arm and marvel at how perfect this feels.

We sit in silence for a while, each of us reading our books. I look over to see Rhys smiling as he reads. I finish my novel and hurl it across the room, not concerned it might hit something.

"That was the most unsatisfactory finish to a book I've read in ages." I cross my arms and lean back against the bedhead.

"That bad?" Rhys questions.

"Yeah. I mean, nah, I should make you read it, and then we can compare notes." My anger shines through.

"Okay."

"Really?" I look at him as he sits next to me, focused on his book.

He doesn't tell me to simmer down, or that it's just a story. He accepts my anger and doesn't question it.

"Yes, you've got great taste in novels," he tells me as he pushes his glasses up his nose. "What didn't you like about this one?"

"It was meant to end in a happily ever after, but it was anything but. It was like false advertising. I wanted them to see how perfect they were together and to actually let go of their pasts and see what was in front of them. I mean, the reader could clearly feel the chemistry, and it's a cop out saying that they've been given strengths they can use when they find their forever person when I think that they are each other's forever person."

"You've got strong feelings about this." Rhys looks at me, but again doesn't try to shut me down.

"I suppose so. And I've just ruined it for you." I chuckle.

"So, it was a romance?" Rhys asks.

"No, a mystery really, but the real mystery is how they didn't end up together. I think the author gets away without the happily ever after because it wasn't billed as a romance, and yet, the romance element was the most believable element of the story. I mean, I'm not the medical one, but I can't see how anyone who's taken a bullet to the shoulder can go on and shoot five guys charging at him using the hand attached to the injured arm."

"Do you rate books, like, review them online?" Rhys asks me.

"Sometimes. Tonight, I'd give it one star, but tomorrow, I'd probably give it three, because it was well written. Can you turn out the light when you've finished?" I ask as I snuggle down into the bed.

"I'm almost done. Sorry if I'm keeping you awake." Rhys goes to close his device, but I tell him to finish his chapter.

"It's okay. It's nice having someone I can talk to." I'm facing the window, my back to him, but I can feel Rhys' gaze on me.

"Do you usually make them leave as soon as they have fulfilled their requirements?" he asks.

"I'm usually the one who gets up to leave." I sigh. "I never bring a guy back to my place—too dangerous."

"Hmm." Rhys carries on reading for a minute or two before he switches off the light and lays back down. "Goodnight."

"Goodnight, and thank you again." I want to give him a kiss to thank him, but I know that's not a good idea.

"You've thanked me enough, I think." We're both now lying on our backs.

"Well, you really have helped me this weekend, and I appreciate it." I take his hand again and give it a squeeze.

"I happen to think your family is just lovely and am having a most enjoyable time." My mouth grows a wide grin again at Rhys' turn of phrase. The thing is, I'm having a most enjoyable time, too.

We both turn on our sides, and I feel his back press against mine. I'm tired, having not slept a lot the night before, and I must drift off easily. As predicted, I wake to find I've removed not only my T-shirt, but I've rolled my knickers down my legs. Drowsily, I looked at my phone and see it's not yet six, so I drift back to sleep, not bothering to redress myself.

I don't recall waking again, but I must do, feeling absolute arousal as I'm being spooned. A hand caresses my breast, twirling my nipple and flicking it, whilst lips suck and lick at the base of my neck. A large penis pokes between my buttocks. I'm sure both of us will later claim we're half asleep, but I feel my bottom move slightly and my legs open, Rhys's cock pressing into my inner folds. We both edge together at the same time as I envelop his cock, and with one thrust, he is balls deep inside me.

The feeling is better than my dreams. His lips have moved from my neck, finding my ear as my head is thrown back in pleasure. He nibbles on the lobe as his fingers trail across my stomach. One of my own hands replaces his in playing with my breasts, rolling my nipples between my fingers and kneading the mounds that seem to have a direct link to my pussy.

We're both groaning and panting, our sounds filling my room like the most amazing symphony, creating a harmony that feels and sounds perfect. I feel Rhys' hand reach down and start stroking my clit. The pressure varies as he thrusts in and out. I don't want this to end. I know I'm half asleep, but any thoughts of not sleeping with a coworker have disappeared, and my body has taken over, ignoring any protests my mind tries to send out. My orgasm is building, and I'm amazed at how good it feels to have Rhys inside me, our bodies moving in sync. All too soon, I explode in ecstasy and feel Rhys pump away as he, too, climaxes. His breathing slows, and I wonder if he is falling asleep again. I can feel him softening inside me, the moisture from our releases trickling down my legs. Suddenly, Rhys pushes me away and shrieks under his breath.

"Oh, Val, I am so sorry," Rhys whispers as if he's just realised what we've done. "I-I was half asleep and... Oh my god, I'm, wow. That was so not planned. I, um, wow. Fuck." I've never seen Rhys as undone as now. He sits up in my bed, his hand raking through his hair. His eyes are as wide as saucers as he comprehends what's just happened.

"Yep, that's what we did. Morning." I roll over and kiss him on the lips. I feel it's the least I can do for waking me up in such a perfect manner. My body feels like jelly, and my brain is beyond processing what we've done. The euphoria is intense; the orgasm was one of the best I've had in my life.

"You're, you're, you're not angry?" He looks at me as if he's about to be sick.

"Angry?" I take a deep breath. "No, not angry. Surprised maybe. I mean, I never thought we'd be so bloody good together."

"It wasn't bad, was it?" Rhys' breathing evens out, and I wonder if some of the happy hormones are hitting his system.

"Not at all." I quirk an eyebrow as I perch on an elbow. "And I am extremely picky. I forgot how nice it was to wake up with someone and be half asleep and feel them arouse you and just become one." That Rhys is the one shocked at what has happened and I'm the one who is calm surprises me. I've held up these boundaries for years and the first time they drop and I break my rule and sleep with a coworker, I'm the one reassuring him.

"You were aroused? You're okay?" he whispers again.

"Relax, would you?" I stroke my hand down his thigh, feeling the hairs standing up as I sweep by them. I enjoy having this effect on him. "A girl would have to be aroused for that monster to slip in so easily. Are you always this edgy post-sex?"

"Well, no, but I mean, usually, it's consensual and, well..." Rhys is still playing with his hair.

"I felt that was consensual, and it was very sensual, and at least I can look Emily in the eye today and tell her that her theory holds."

"Are you going to be able to look at me at work?" Rhys' voice is one of pain.

"What, and not want to rip your clothes off? I'm going to have to be, aren't I?" It's easier for me to laugh and joke and not face that I've just had some of the best sex of my life, and it wasn't planned, and it looks like Rhys doesn't want any more.

"Fuck, that was nice, like, wow." Rhys smiles as he shakes his head, his brain finally catching up to what we did.

"The euphoria's washing over you too?" I ask.

"Indeed." Rhys chuckles. "No. Contraception?" Fear washes across Rhys's face.

"I've got an IUD. I assume you're clean? You're the first guy who has come inside me without protection for..." I pause to think. "Fuck. You're the first guy ever. Congratulations!"

"It's not a title I'll boast about." Rhys laughs as he rubs my shoulder. "But, yeah, it's the first time I've ever had sex without a condom, too."

"Perhaps I should get a plaque made for your desk, or a trophy or something," I joke.

"Are you two coming down for breakfast?" Mum knocks at our door. "I know you're awake. Your father and I heard you downstairs. Your father's still smiling."

"Mother," I groan as she opens the door, and I pull the sheet over my breasts.

"Well, I lost my bet." She doesn't seem sad about this at all, her face radiating joy.

"What bet?" Rhys asks.

"I thought Val would bring a decoy home. Giles was convinced you're the real deal. Congratulations, you two." Mum shuts the door, and I can hear her humming as she makes her way downstairs.

"I am so sorry that I've put you in a shit position. I know it's only until Monday. Then we go back to being colleagues, and that's that. If you want to find an excuse to head home, I will understand." I find it hard to look Rhys in the eye, for fear of my true feelings showing.

If I wasn't convinced before this morning that Rhys is perfect for me, then the sex has helped seal the deal. I won't lie. Rhys isn't like the guy from Legal Aid. He's fit in so well with my family, and me with his, that perhaps the universe is telling me to ditch my rules and give him a go.

"I can't do that to you." Rhys closes his eyes and lets out a breath. "Look, I'm excited about spending time with your brothers today. We must be the only doctors and lawyers in the land who don't play golf, but I understand Giles has something special planned. You have fun with your mother and the girls, and remember, I've already booked the first dance with you tonight."

"Not the last?" I ask.

"I might be swept off my feet by a dashing doctor, who knows?" he jokes, but as I look at him, I see his smile doesn't meet his eyes.

"Thanks for making me laugh and not running after this morning." I'm sincere in my words. I want to tell him it's no longer an act for me and suggest we see where things go.

"If I knew we were going to be that good together, perhaps I would have put out sooner." Rhys quips, a twinkle in his eye.

I toss a pillow at him as I throw a T-shirt over my head and head for the bathroom. As strange as things are, he is an outstanding choice for my weekend partner, and I know I do not want Monday to come. I know I'm still swept up in the sex hormones from this morning. I can't make a call now, but I'll see how I feel after my day with the girls, a day I'm dreading.

After Rhys has stepped into the shower and I'm dressed, I make my way downstairs and hear the kettle whistling, hinting at a fresh pot of tea.

"I thought you might have saved water and showered together like we did." My parents gaze at each other as if they're newlyweds as I walk into the kitchen. "Honestly, love, I don't think I could have chosen a doctor who would be more suited to you than Rhys is. I wish I had a camera on me last night to snap both of you sitting up in bed reading together. It was just perfect. And that chest." Mum fans herself with her hand. "I can see what the appeal is—Charlie, he obviously works out, unlike some."

"Thanks, Mum. Happy anniversary, you two. I assume it started with a bang by the grins on your faces." I'm almost glad I slept through their morning sex. If they heard us, no doubt we would have heard them if we'd been awake.

"You can't at least wonder where you got your sex drive from? I'm just glad Rhys makes you as happy as Charlie's made me for the last forty-plus years. He's definitely a keeper, like your father." Mum and Dad share a kiss as Dad pours me a cup of tea.

Being away from my family, I've forgotten what their brand of love looks and feels like. I've surrounded myself with people trying to break away from failed relationships. Maybe I need to focus on the things my parents and siblings do to maintain their relationships and believe that I, too, can have what they have.

# 16

## Rhys

I'M STANDING IN THE BATHROOM, MY HANDS PRESSED against the bench as I look at the image of the man staring back at me in the mirror. The same man who just had his cock inside Valerie Hartman. Bare. I've never gone bare before. Fuck, I've never had sex like that before. I've also never woken up fucking someone.

One minute, I'm dreaming that Val's telling me the fiction we've created has been an audition, and I've passed with flying colours, the next, I'm balls deep inside of her.

She felt, I mean, amazing is an overused word. Phenomenal doesn't even seem to cut it. She felt like home, like I was meant to be there. It wasn't long, drawn-out sex, and it wouldn't surprise me if I lasted merely a few pumps, but feeling her pussy contract around me, drawing out my cum, is something I will not forget in a while, if ever.

My first thought was that neither of us had consented. I'd pushed myself onto her, well, into her, I suppose, without her permission. Val didn't seem to mind, though. Call it the endorphins, but she was so relaxed after it that I don't even think she noticed that she walked to the bathroom half-naked.

The image of her tossing the pillow at me as she stood there naked is now imprinted on my brain. The way her breasts teased upwards, her nipples pointing to my eyes. The curve of her hips, and that smile that engulfed her face. It felt as though she was seeing me for the first time, and she didn't mind what she saw.

From reliving how we screwed, my mind reminds me that I am now utterly screwed. One taste of Val is hardly enough, and we didn't even kiss. I mean, that peck on the lips from her was divine, but it's not how I want to kiss her. I want to show her how special she is to me.

Our day will be busy, Val with the women at the salon, and me with the boys doing who knows what, but I want to find time to talk to her, to tell her I want to give us a go, that I think we are perfect for each other, and she is my person. Boyd told me last night not to shave this morning and to wear old clothes. I don't think he realises some of the things I wear on *Serenity* most people wouldn't be seen dead in, but I have some shorts and a T-shirt I don't mind getting dirty with me. After a quick shower, I dress and make my way downstairs.

"Here he is." Hillary moves straight for me, grasping my cheeks in her hands before removing one to replace it with a kiss. "Now, we don't believe that Val's property and you need to ask our permission or anything, but please just know that Charlie and I both adore you and are thrilled to see the two of you so happy together."

"Mum." Val cries as she leans forward and places her head on the bench, lightly tapping it. "I keep telling you, it's early days, and there'll probably be so much Rhys can tolerate about me. He'll go running for the hills as soon as we get back to Brisbane."

"Oh, hush." Hillary moves back to the cupboard and reaches for a mug before pouring me a cup of tea. "You don't seriously agree with her, do you, Rhys?"

"Hillary." Charlie sounds gruff as he lowers his newspaper and glares at his wife over his glasses. "Now, what time is everyone heading out? I need me some peace and quiet."

"We're due at the salon at ten," Val groans. She's told me before how much she hates what she calls 'girly stuff'.

"Boyd said to be ready about now." I glance down at my watch just as Boyd and Giles enter the kitchen.

"Happy anniversary, parentals, and Happy Valentine's Day to all the lovers. Oh, wait, that's all of us this year." Boyd high fives his sister as she rolls her eyes.

"Sure you don't want to come, Dad?" Giles asks as Charlie shakes his head.

"I need some peace. It's been one noise after another this morning." Charlie winks at me as he says this, and I try to stifle a grin.

I'm glad to be leaving in some ways, because I don't enjoy hearing Val talk about impending breakups and putting herself down. I want her to see herself as I see her, a remarkable woman who is allowed to feel love and be loved in return. Her parents are thrilled about us, but, clearly, she still has her doubts. I'll have to try to win her over in other ways.

"You jump in the front." Boyd slaps my back as we get into Giles' SUV. "We've got to pick up Hen and Ken. I'll sit in the middle."

"I don't think Henry will like that." Giles looks at his brother through the rearview mirror.

It's a short drive to Henry and Ken's place. We stay in the car as Giles beeps the horn. Boyd is about to jump out when the front door of the townhouse swings open and Henry and Ken appear. Both nod at each other before reaching down and pretending to zip up their flies. Giles shakes his head as Boyd giggles at their antics. It strikes me that the other two don't know that this is really Henry and Ken's bachelor do, their last hurrah before their wedding tonight.

Ken threatens to sit on Henry's lap unless Boyd moves from the middle seat, which he reluctantly does when they start making out.

"Sorry, it's just a special day for us, that's all." Henry strokes the side of Ken's face.

Val's told me about how they met on this day ten years ago before Ken ran away from him at the gala ball. She is surrounded by amazing examples of love in her parents and brothers, and it surprises me that she can't see herself having the same experience. I know my views of marriage are skewed by my parents and their activities, but even so, I know I'd like to find someone to spend my life with.

"No! Laser Tag?" Boyd's voice shoots up two octaves, and he bounces in his seat as Giles pulls up outside what looks like a large warehouse.

"Christian's meeting us here, plus a few guys from work. Sorry, Rhys, I don't know any lawyers to invite to join us." Giles turns to the guys in the back before looking at me.

"No worries." I laugh, amazed that Giles even thought about me.

"Christian is Hen's best mate," Boyd says from the back, and I realise I'm not meant to know who he is, despite Val telling me only because of the upcoming nuptials.

We head inside, and I'm introduced to people whose names I've already forgotten. One of them works with Boyd and does this every week. Boyd seems to think that's a great idea. Val told me Boyd is like a little kid, but until I met him, I didn't realise how true that was. He's more than his jokes and antics, though, and I feel a strong connection to him.

I'll be upset if this thing with Val ends on Monday, but apart from missing her, I'll miss her family. Charlie and I sat by the pool yesterday afternoon and shared a beer. He told me about finding the house and how they turned it into a home. As much as he loves it, though, he's ready to move somewhere smaller, despite losing the memories. He all but said the house could be Val's for a very reasonable price.

The thought of living in such a stunning family home is nice, but the thought of living there with Val is something else. My heart races as I allow myself to dream of a future here. I still have my doubts that this morning meant the same thing to her that it did to me, but the fact she didn't send me packing makes me wonder if maybe she is coming around to the possibility of a future together.

"Okay, so listen up." Our instructor gives us a briefing and shows us how our kit works. We're playing as individuals, and our task is to capture a flag. I've not played this before, but I've played plenty of Capture the Flag in my youth. Who would have thought home-schooling get-togethers would come in handy later in life? A wry grin creeps across my face as I imagine my parents complaining about the capitalism that is evident in this place. To me, it seems like a lot of fun, and people need to make money however they can, and I'd much rather be doing this in air-conditioning this time of year.

It's dark when we're let inside the maze, and despite the loud music, we need to creep around in order to find the flag. We're given thirty seconds to find a starting point. People scurry off, but I wait just inside the door, wanting to hold back a little. My plan is to be behind everyone so they don't see me coming. Sure, it's a risk, but none of us know where the flag is. Someone might stumble across it by running ahead now, but I stick to my plan.

A siren sounds, showing our ten minutes have started. I creep forward, crouched low as I look around the first corner. I stifle a giggle as Henry and Ken stand there making out. It's clear they haven't planned on finding the flag, but I make their vests buzz as I shoot them. They don't break their kiss, but Henry gives me a thumbs up.

I hear a scuffle ahead and am about to take out Boyd's colleague when I see he shoots at someone ahead of me. Holding back, I follow from a distance, watching him move unnoticed around the course, neutralising Hartmans and other colleagues alike. Boyd swears as he's shot, drawing attention to the guy in front of me. I see Giles turn, and just as he shoots at the guy I'm shadowing, I land a shot on him, causing his vest to light up. So far, I've counted seven casualties, so there are two more people out here with me. I'm unsure how many minutes we have left. I spy someone ahead of me, who darts back into the same area as me, except he has his back to me.

Crouching low, I see Christian head around the corner, aiming at the guy ahead of me and hitting him. He doesn't see me, and I land the final blow. Now, I just need to find the flag. I'm pretty sure my calculations are correct, and everyone has been accounted for. There can't be much time left. I'm darting down passages and wondering if I'm doubling back on myself half the time. I then see it, a fluorescent orange flag with the business's logo in it poking out the side of the wall. Just as I grab at it, a siren sounds, the room flooding with light.

"Well done." Boyd slaps my shoulder. With the room not in darkness and the special effects unlit, it's not a challenge to find our way out.

We all grab a bottle of water and ready ourselves for the next round. Giles gives me a nod and a smile, recognising my tactics, but the others seem to be too busy talking amongst themselves.

We manage five more rounds; me winning another three to make me the victor for the day. There's no ill feeling amongst these people. We've all just had an exciting and fun morning. As much as I can't imagine

Max or Katherine enjoying laser tag, I can see Val loving it. I get the impression she's competitive enough that she wouldn't do a Henry and Ken and simply use it as a chance to make out, even though that sounds pretty amazing to me.

We head to a bar for lunch. Christian joins us, but the other guys head off to do their own thing, all commenting that they're looking forward to the gala tonight. I'm waiting for the inquisition about my intentions with their sister, but it never comes.

"Val would have loved this morning." Boyd shakes his head.

"And she would have found a way to beat us all." Giles takes a swig of his beer before pointing the neck at Boyd.

"Rhys might have been able to distract her the way Ken distracted me." Henry's face lights up as he stares at Ken, both of them silently communicating with their gazes.

"I suspect her competitiveness would have won through." I play with the label on the bottle, picking at the corners.

"Well, I think if anyone could distract her, it would be you." Boyd nudges my shoulder, and I force a smile.

I'd like to think I could, but there's no certainty. I want to speak to her and clear the air after this morning, but I'm not sure if there will be time.

"You're good for her, Rhys." Giles spins his bottle in his palms. "I mean, sure, we've tried to push colleagues onto her over the years, but I don't think any of them would be as perfect for her as you are. She needs someone who lets her shine. I mean, last night, we saw how you carried on with Boyd and Emily. I suppose what I'm saying is, you fit in with the family, and that's important."

I don't know what to say to Giles as I don't want to break our façade and tell them all it's a giant act. I know I'm not acting one little bit, but I suspect Val is. She's grown up amongst this family that lives and breathes love, and she can't seem to accept that she, too, is worthy of experiencing this for herself. I want to give it to her and show her that we can be amazing together, but I don't think she's there yet. Sometimes, I wonder if she'll ever be there, but I can't think about that now. I'm out with the guys, and we've got a gala ball to prepare for.

"Yeah, get rid of the beard." Henry's eyes twinkle as he tells the barber to give him a clean shave.

"Don't you fucking dare." Ken swivels from the seat next to Henry, his barber fortunately not near his head with scissors.

"I'm only joking." Hen reaches across and takes Ken's hand. "But Boyd is clearing off that bum fluff he's trying to call a beard."

Henry said he was in charge of things this afternoon and has arranged for us to have a trip to a barber. I had my hair trimmed during the week, but I am always up for a shave with a cut-throat razor and a hot towel. I love the way the brothers bounce off each other, Ken clearly being included as a Hartman after so many years with them.

Myf and I have bantered from time to time, but nothing like these guys. It's one of the reasons I want more than two children.

The barbers get to work on Henry and Ken. Boyd is flopped next to me on a comfy sofa, with Giles sitting on a bench reading a magazine about MotorX.

"What about you, Gilbo?" Boyd kicks at Giles' foot, which stretches out in front of him. "You shaving or growing a beard?"

"I haven't had a beard since uni." Giles narrows his eyes, still looking at the magazine.

"Yeah, it would probably be grey like the sides of your hair." Boyd chuckles.

Giles drops the magazine to his lap and huffs out a long breath. "Jealous much?"

"Nah, not really. Grey pubes would be pretty off-putting, though." Boyd doesn't know when to stop, but it is amusing listening to him. "It would be like fucking a grandad."

Giles doesn't take the bait, simply smiling as he picks up the magazine again. Before long, he's called to a chair.

"Aw, look at her." Boyd shows me his phone and a photo of Issy covered in something tomatoey. "Nonna's cooked her pasta."

"She's gorgeous." I smile, my heart warming at the sight of this besotted father. "Val said it had been a rough road for you and Emily."

"Yeah." He strokes his chin thoughtfully. "To think, five years ago, she tried to tell me our marriage was over and I needed to find someone else. I mean, it's been a rough road, but we've learnt so much about each other."

"My sister and brother-in-law have been trying for a few years. They're talking about fostering now."

"Good for them." Boyd nods, still looking at the photo of his daughter that he has just made his screen saver on his phone. "We're just lucky things went so well last cycle. We've got an embryo on ice, but even if that cycle doesn't work, I don't think we'll do any more IVF."

Henry and Ken are finished, and Boyd and I are instructed to change places with them. The barber isn't chatty, which suits me. I need some quiet time to recharge. I've had a lovely day with these Hartman men. They're all besotted with their partners, and they expect me to be as besotted with Val. The truth is, I am, but I don't think Val can see this.

I recognise my shyness contributes to my piss poor communication, but it really isn't helping the situation. I need to get Val by herself and tell her exactly how I'm feeling and hope she is feeling the same way.

The rhythmic sound of the razor across my stubble relaxes me. The barber is methodical and precise, which is fortunate, as he has a sharp blade in the vicinity of my jugular. The shave doesn't take long, much less time than if I was shaving myself. I'm left to sit there with a warm towel around my face and neck, before the barber returns and rubs a moisturiser in. I think I catch a whiff of citrus notes, but he assures me it's a neutral scent.

Boyd is finishing off with his barber, his beard and hair both being trimmed. I wonder how Val and the women are going. Val told me she's not keen on beauty treatments. I had to laugh when she said the payoff for not having to style her hair every morning was having it cut every four weeks. She's been looking forward to spending time with her family, especially Emily, and I hope she can spend the day relaxing before tonight. I'm still worried our unexpected sex might see her run for the hills, but we'll see.

I can only hope we'll spend the night dancing cheek to cheek after

I've been able to explain my feelings for this amazing woman. I need to tell her how much she means to me and how special she is. I just hope we have time before the gala.

# 17

# Val

"THIS BRINGS BACK MEMORIES OF MY WEDDING, YOU AND ME getting our fingers and toes done." Emily grabs my arm from the chair next to me. Of course, I hadn't known it was going to be her wedding day. That was a surprise for later on. "We'll have to do it for you, too, Val. Just don't let Rhys get away from you. I mean, you two are just perfect together."

"I can't see myself getting married anytime soon, and you know I rarely do these girly things." Because I didn't mind having a bit of colour on my toes, I suffer through having someone play with my feet, but I hate painting them myself. Even so, I'd rather sit here with a book than talk with people, even if they are my family.

"Just you wait. As soon as Rhys pops the question... I mean, you're the last of my children..." Mum flicks through the colour samples, looking for the perfect ruby red for her fingers and toes.

"Ah, Mum, what about Henry and Ken?" I roll my eyes. I've already chosen a colour called Nude Glow. It took me all of thirty seconds.

"Can you imagine them organising a wedding together?" Mum laughs, putting down another ring of samples. "Nothing would get done. They'd be fighting over colour schemes and where to best hang the fairy lights and which brother would be his best man!"

"That would be my Boyd, surely." Emily looks up from her samples. "I mean, Hen was best man for Giles. Giles was best man for Boyd, so it must be Boyd's turn." Emily had chosen a purple to match the streak that ran through her hair.

I was glad I was not going to be near Emily when all was revealed tonight. It was fun keeping Henry and Ken's secret. Mum and Emily continued to speculate on what Henry and Ken would organise for a wedding—something swanky with amazing food and everyone dressed up to the nines. Well, I hoped tonight would satisfy that.

Bridget was comparing different pale pink shades of polish and had narrowed it down to three contenders.

"Well, they were in the marquee yesterday after work fiddling with things. I suggested they take yesterday off to help, but, no, they left it to us girls, as usual." Mum has a glitter sample in one hand and a gloss in the other. Emily convinces her to go with the glitter. "Bridget, I owe Giles money, too. He was right, and Rhys and Val are the real deal and not a decoy for the weekend."

"I am not getting involved in your schemes, Hills." Bridget tosses one of the samples back, further narrowing her choices to two colours, both of which looked the same to me. "I suspect that if you hadn't suggested the possibility, Giles would have already been thinking it, and he'd be losing the bet." Bridget settles on a colour and hands the sample to the beautician who retrieves the polish from the shelf. "I wish you would all stop picking on poor Val. She's a godsend in the school holidays, and Millie and Mia adore their aunt."

"Thanks, Bridget. Where are they, anyway? I thought they were part of this girls' thing?" I sit back with my arms folded. Mum and Emily are going first, then Bridget and me. I should have brought a book with me.

"No, just hair and 'minimal makeup' as per their father. I'm going to pick them up after this. Giles is finding it hard to take now that they're growing up," Bridget muses.

"You still haven't told me about my finger theory, Val." Emily is anything if not persistent, relaxing with her feet being pampered.

"What?" Bridget asks as she sips the water with cucumber slices in it we've been provided with. I'd prefer a Mimosa or Bloody Mary to be honest.

"Em thinks that if a guy has long fingers, he's hung," I tell her.

"Giles is hung like a racehorse." Bridget flips through a magazine, but she's not actually reading any of it.

"Add Charlie, too, Em. Although his fingers are not as long as his sons', he has kept me very satisfied for over forty years now. Now, don't we all wish Ken was here, too?" Mum laughs as I shake my head.

"No, Mother, not at all. This is just disgraceful talking about men as if they're stud animals." I try to sound indignant, but the reality is, I know once Mum gets going, there will be no stopping her.

"Just wait, Val, it's all us married women have to talk about." She wiggles her eyebrows, and I shake my head.

"Speak for yourself, Hills." Bridget tosses the magazine back onto the pile. "Giles would be mortified if he knew we were talking about his penis. So, what did you get Charlie for your anniversary?" Thank heavens for Bridget changing the subject.

"Well, for our thirtieth, I got a Brazilian wax job, and whilst Charlie liked it, he said it made little difference to him. I thought about a clit or nipple piercing, but I'm not into pain, so I got him some nice lingerie and a couple of new toys to add to our collection." And we're back where we started. I blow out a long breath.

"Oh my god, Mum. I now know why I moved away." I shake my head, and Mum laughs.

"And we all miss you, Val. We really do and would love it if you moved back." There are tears in Mum's eyes as she talks, and I know she means what she says. I miss my family, too, as this weekend is showing me.

As much as I pretend I'd love to sit here with a book, I love the Hartman women. I loved my time living with Giles and Bridget when I first moved to Brisbane, and I miss my nieces something fierce.

"I know, Mum. I know."

The day would have gone much quicker if we went to a dedicated nail salon, but the Hartmans have used Gloria's Hair and Beauty since I was a child. I loved that they'd created a space for the four of us to sit and talk whilst our hands and feet are tended to.

The beauticians are quiet and don't interrupt us at all. I want to give them a huge tip to thank them for their professionalism.

"So, Emily"—Mum didn't bother pretending to read a magazine as my heels were buffed and legs moisturised—"is there a time limit on the embryo you've got on ice?"

"Not really." Emily sits back in the comfortable chair, her legs crossed. "I mean, Isobel's birth was a little traumatic, and I don't think I'm ready to go again just yet, but Boyd and I thought that once she's two, we might think about transferring our little Emby."

"Three years is a good age gap." Mum nods. "Two was good between Giles and Henry. If things had gone to plan, there would have been three between Boyd, and Val too, but Val had other ideas."

"I didn't gestate for twenty-one months, Mum." I laugh.

"No, but it took us twelve months to conceive you, my darling." Mum has a wistful look on her face as she looks towards the ceiling, clearly remembering back to those days.

"Giles had taken a couple of months to conceive, Henry was straight away, and Boyd was two months from memory, but Val was stubborn." It shouldn't have surprised me that I was meticulously planned, even if those plans didn't follow the schedule my mother would have liked. "You know I would have loved a fifth child, but your father put his foot down. In the end, I relented and agreed to him having the snip. I wasn't getting any younger after all."

"Did Giles get the snip?" I turn to Bridget before flicking my head to Emily, who's let out an audible gasp.

"It's okay, Em." Bridget leans over and smiles at her. I can't work out what I've said. "We would have loved more children. I, well, I had a miscarriage before Millie came along, and Mia's birth was so traumatic that they almost lost me and saved me by removing my uterus. So, there were no more kids for us." Bridget shrugs her shoulders, ever the pragmatist.

"I'm sorry. I shouldn't have asked that." My brows knit together.

I complain about my mother interfering, and yet, sometimes, I wonder if I'm as bad.

"It's okay. I told Emily when she and Boyd were first trying, but I've never shared it with you or Hills. And that's wrong of me."

"I don't think it's a case of right or wrong." Mum holds Emily's hand as they sit together, waiting for the next part of our visit to the salon. "I know I can be overenthusiastic at times. I do it out of love, but it doesn't make it right. It's something I've been trying to work on for many years now."

Seeing my mum and brothers' wives so content with things, even though they haven't gone to plan, makes me wonder what my plan actually is with Rhys. I can't kid myself anymore that I haven't fallen head over heels in love with him, but I need to work out a way of telling him and figuring out if he wants the same. For all I know, he may be looking forward to Monday and getting away from all of this.

I'm not sure if we'll have time to talk before the gala, but I hope we have time after, because I think we could create something special together. As much as I dreaded this day at the salon with the girls, it reminds me what a beautiful family I have and makes me realise how much I miss them, living so far away.

MILLIE AND MIA join us for hair and makeup, as does Ken's sister, Dipti. Fortunately, there were more hair stylists than beauticians, but it still took time to glam everyone up. Millie has her nose in a book. She reminds me of myself at her age. Mia explains in great detail the intricacies of her latest piano piece and how she was playing football at school.

It was after five when we all finished. We'd have just enough time to get home and get dressed before taking the family photos Henry had arranged and making our way to the marquee. I thought I'd have time for a leisurely bath, but it was not meant to be.

Mum and I were quiet on our drive home from the salon. My mind was filled with memories of previous gala balls, from the first one where I'd been not much older than Millie and had worn my Doc Marten boots, the second one where I'd danced the night away and, despite all the good-looking single guys present, still hadn't managed to pick up, to the last one where I spent a lot of the night comforting Emily who was trying unsuccessfully to break up with Boyd.

Tonight would be different. I couldn't wait to see Rhys in a tux. The thought of holding him close as we dance and stroking the back of his neck as I take in his sandalwood scent saw me smile.

"You're thinking about Rhys again, aren't you?" Mum smiled at me as we stopped at a red light.

"Yeah," I reply honestly. "I am. He's..." I pause, trying to find the right words. "He's amazing."

Amazing is only part of it. I can't tell my mum that I've fallen for him when I haven't even told Rhys. He's the breeze to my sails, the cheese to my cracker, and, well, my biggest cheerleader and supporter. It shouldn't matter that we work together. He's not the type of person who would make things unbearable if things don't work out between us. But then again, I can't see things not working out. It's a strange realisation, and not one that I've ever thought I'd entertain.

I look at my phone. There's been no messages from him today. There won't be time to talk before the gala, and I don't want to send a text telling him we need to talk. If I received a text like that, I'd fear the worst. Perhaps during the gala, we'll find time to have a chat—perhaps escape to the pool house or inside or something.

Mum pulls up in the garage attached to the house. There's already a flurry of activity happening with caterers present, and I can hear the band doing a sound check as I climb out of the sedan.

We walked inside to see Dad and Rhys nursing a glass of scotch, Rhys with a book in his hand, and Dad with the paper and a pen. Usually, he's completed the crossword by now, so he must have been busy this afternoon with the various people helping get ready for tonight.

"Hey, how was your day?" I ask Rhys as he stood and bit his bottom lip, his eyes wide as he stared at me.

"Good. Great. Your brothers are amazing." Rhys is wearing black pants and a white T-shirt. It's an amazing look on him. Dad follows Mum, telling us he's going to help her slip into her gown.

"How was your day?" I smile, perching myself on the arm of the chair Rhys is sitting in.

"We played laser tag with some of their mates from the hospital and then went to lunch, followed by the barber." Rhys can't take his eyes off me, and I feel them trailing up and down my body. We stand, and I take his hand as we ascend the stairs together to get ready. "The barber was Ken's idea, but I haven't had a close shave like that in ages." Rhys rubs his face with his hand, and I have to stroke a finger down to find that it is indeed smooth.

"I thought Ken liked Henry's beard?"

"Yeah, we heard all about it." Rhys lets out a chuckle. "Hen just had a trim. Don't worry."

"You look..." Rhys swallows, and I swear his Adam's apple bobs more than normal. "You look incredible, and as much as I want to kiss you, I don't want to mess up your hair or makeup." Rhys plants a kiss on my forehead.

Rhys uses Boyd's old room to dress in. I almost tell him to stay in mine, and we'll get ready together, but his shirt and jacket are already hanging next door. Despite not being terribly relaxed, I stick my breasts to my chest with the bunny tape I had been sold, put on my sexy thong, and throw my dress over my head. The zip is at the side and easy to fasten. I sit on the edge of my bed and buckle my shoes.

I stand and look at myself in the full-length mirror that hangs behind my door. There's a glow that I think can only be explained by the way Rhys makes me feel, so cherished and desired. I need to find out if this is all an act though, or if I am reading things correctly, and he likes me as much as I seem to like him.

There's a tap at my door.

"Come in." I clear my throat after my croaky response and stand back as the door opens.

"Wow." I twirl on the spot, loving the feel of the organza floating back against my legs as I stop. "You look spectacular, I mean, wow!" Rhys almost whispers as he takes me in.

"Look at you, too." I walk towards him and brush an invisible speck of lint off his collar. "I mean, I love a dinner suit. It's the pleats on the shirt, and you fill it out well. That red tie, I don't know... It makes your eyes almost bluer, if that is possible."

"I never realised you knew I have blue eyes." These eyes stare into mine. Rhys must be able to see the effect he has on me, or at least hear my heartbeat as it thunders away.

"Of course. They're beautiful." I break away before I get carried away, knowing we're due downstairs any minute now. "Here, I almost forgot. Happy Valentine's Day." I hand him a box that contains a hand-turned pen with a heart-shaped inlay along one side. "I saw this and thought of you. I understand the wood is from an old ship, which made the pen that bit more special in my eyes."

"Thank you," Rhys murmurs, his mouth open as he inspects the pen closely. "Thank you so much. It's, it's just perfect. Here. Happy Valentine's Day." Rhys pulls a small velvet box done up with a ribbon out of his pants pocket.

My heart stops. Rhys and I haven't mentioned marriage or anything like that. My fingers shake as I undo the ribbon and snap the lid. Nestled inside is a pair of stunning long earrings with a deep-red stone on the ends.

"Oh my gosh," I gush. "They're perfect. Here, can you help me put them in?"

"They match quite well, even if I say so myself." Rhys takes the earrings from my shaking fingers and slides them through the holes in my lobes. I'd forgotten to bring any jewellery with me.

Rhys stands behind me as I close the door again to look in the mirror. "Oh, Rhys, they are stunning. Not too loud, but a little bit of sparkle."

"I wanted you to have something to remember this little adventure we had. I hope it's been as fun for you as it has for me." Rhys' hands rest on my shoulders, and he gives them a slight squeeze before removing them and opening the door.

My heart sinks. This is still an act for him. He knows we have an expiration date. Heck, he set it himself when we first talked about a fake relationship. I blink away the tears that are threatening to fall.

"Val, Rhys?" Giles' booming voice can be heard from downstairs.

"Come on. It was a good idea of Hen to organise a photographer. Sounds like the others are here." I take a deep breath and head down the stairs, one hand on the rail, the other holding my dress. I don't risk touching Rhys. I need to step back so I can protect my heart. Fiction is not reality.

# 18

## Rhys

My hands shake as I tie the red silk tie around my neck. When Hillary and Val walked into the lounge after their day at the salon, my heartbeat quickened, and my jaw dropped open. Val rarely wears a lot of makeup, and I was almost expecting a full-on glam up, like women I'd previously dated, but she looked so natural. If I didn't know any better, I'd have assumed she was just wearing some mascara and lip gloss. Her face glowed, though. I had no idea what product they've put in her hair, but it just shines.

Walking into her room and seeing her in her red gown almost undid me. The expanse of skin down her back that I'll get to caress as we dance later and the hint of side boob had the blood rushing to my cock.

I spent an afternoon during the week browsing jewellery stores and found the earrings I gave her in a vintage store. Val wouldn't like anything flashy, but I wanted something delicate and subtle. I made a good choice, and the earrings look amazing.

The pen Val gave me is tucked inside my pocket. To realise Val had observed that I still write with a fountain pen and had found a stunning handmade item that had maritime links really touched me. That she knew I have blue eyes gave me further hope that she's noticed more about me.

"Hillary and Charlie, if you sit here, and Charlie, if you take the baby..." The photographer directs us all as we gather in the lounge room.

I stand to the side. "Come on, Rhys, in you get." Hillary hands Isobel to Charlie and tries to wave me to stand behind Val.

"No, you have some with just the family first," I try to object, but Hillary is having none of it. "I'm sure they can airbrush me out," I whisper in Val's ear.

I can't see her response, but she squeezes my hand as it rests on her waist.

The photographer is quick, having decided already who was going to stand where to get the best shots. It feels natural to stand with Val as she grips my jacket lapels and gazes into my eyes. I could almost swear she wasn't acting.

Mia has the job of presenting her grandparents with a gift from the family for a week away on a secluded island.

"Let me know if I owe you anything for the weekend," I say to Val as we make our way to the marquee.

"Don't be silly." Val swats her hand in the air. I wish her hand was on me.

Her words sting. I want to be part of the weekend with her and part of her family. The hope that this is more to Val than she has let on evaporates. It would appear it is nothing more than an act.

A park and ride system is in place, and the first busload of guests start stepping off the coach as we enter the large tent. The decorations are gorgeous. Fairy lights hang from above with red hearts strung to silver ribbon dangling from the ceiling. There is a bar to the side, a stage at the front with room for dancing, and some tables and chairs for those who prefer to sit.

"This is gorgeous, Val." I lead her to a tall table near the bar. "I'd almost forgotten how lovely Cassowary Point is."

"Did you live here for long?" Val asks me, looking around the marquee. I can't tell if she was looking for someone or something like a glass of champagne.

"A while, until Uncle Derek died. I'm happy to be back again. I've still got a few clients up here and try to get up several times a year. If I'd planned things better, I should have tacked a few days on this trip." Waiters appear with trays of drinks, but they head in the direction away from us. I feel like heading to the bar, as I could really do with something to distract me, even though I'm enjoying talking to Val.

"I honestly don't know how to thank you for this weekend." Val looks at me with soft eyes. "I mean, I've had the loveliest time with you. I'll almost be sad when Monday comes around."

"Really?" I say almost too quickly.

"Yeah, but I know, the contract was only until the sixteenth, and it was probably a good idea that you suggested an end date."

I want to tell her that there doesn't need to be an end date, and I'd be happy to carry on and see where things go, but we're interrupted. Instead, I squeeze Val's arm before grabbing a glass of sparkling wine for us both as the server comes past.

"Mate!" Boyd grabs my hand as he and Emily come towards us. "Gee, she scrubs all right, too. I hardly recognised my own sister and thought about hitting on her until I realised who she was."

"My offer from a few weeks ago stands. Emily will get the best legal representation money can't buy." Val rolls her eyes. It seems to be a Hartman thing to do. I noticed Giles and Henry both rolling their eyes at various stages today, too.

"Settle down." Boyd chuckles. "Did you know her dress has..." Boyd slides his hands up inside some strategically placed slits in his wife's gown and rolls his eyes as he fondles her breasts in public. "I am one lucky man, almost as lucky as my new best mate, Rhys. Did he tell you he won laser tag? Giles is not happy."

"It was pure luck," I try to deflect.

"Who's got Issy?" Val asks.

"Mum's over in the house with her. I gave her a good feed, and she should settle soon." Emily takes a sip of her wine. "You two look so perfect together. It's practically making me cry seeing my best friend so happy after all these years. Sorry, I know it's the hormones, but honestly, you two are made for each other, and I'm so glad to have met you this weekend, Rhys. If I had to part with a best friend who had found a new best friend, I'm so glad it's you."

"Thanks, Em. I'm sorry you got lumbered with my stinky brother,"

Val scoffs. We laugh, and I appreciate my arm around Val's shoulders. It feels natural and, well, perfect.

"Do you really want to go there, stinky?" Boyd dips his head as if he's looking at Val over invisible glasses.

The band starts up, and I take the opportunity to move to the dance floor to hold Val close and move to the music. She's an incredible dancer, light on her feet, and she feels just perfect against my body. We could be the only ones here, and we wouldn't know, as our focus is on each other. The air is electric with possibility, and despite Val mentioning our expiry date, I can still feel something special between us. I just hope she does, too.

It's the not knowing what she's thinking that gets to me though, and I can feel myself being swept up in the fantasy again. If only it wasn't too loud to talk.

After a few numbers, I suggest we look at the silent auction items and place some bids. It's quieter in this corner of the marquee, but not quiet enough to hold a private conversation. A local artist has crafted a glass sculpture of an anatomical heart that looks as though it is so full, it's bursting. It's called *Overflowing Love*, and I can see Val has taken a shine to it.

"I don't know what people will pay for it, but it says it's worth $500, so I might just bid that," Val mumbles to no one in particular, her fingers tracing the arteries and veins.

"You like it, don't you?" I place a hand on her shoulder as she examines the piece.

"I do. I mean, I'm not sure why."

I'm hoping the reason is that she recognises the overflowing nature of love coming from her own heart. "Sometimes, things speak to people, and no one knows why, and it's best not to question ourselves. Good luck."

I fill out several bids myself on various items. It's a worthy cause, after all.

"Don't forget, the big auction is still to come. I understand there is a signed football or something." Val and I had both discovered we did not appreciate football or adorning our office walls with sports memorabilia.

I take a deep breath as the band announces it's going on a break. "So, Monday…"

"Yes." Val pats my arm. "Don't worry. I won't get all clingy or anything. I know the deal."

"There you are." Henry comes to grab Val and tells her they are on.

"Good luck." I watch her walk away with her brother after I've left a kiss on her cheek.

It may have been a brief conversation, but at least I now know where I stand. She seems convinced that Monday is the end day for us. One of Myf's mantras is 'Don't cry because it's over, smile because it happened'. I'm not sure I'll be able to do this with Val, though.

I see Boyd and Emily standing near the stage and head over to join them as Henry appears on the stage.

"Ladies, gentlemen, and lovers beyond the binary. Can I have your attention?" He clears his throat, forgetting to remove the microphone from in front of his mouth. His nerves make me smile. "Thanks. Um, for those who don't know me, I'm Henry Hartman, second son behind Giles, but I'm still ahead of Boyd, and no one remembers Valerie anyway, do they? I mean, she's not a doctor or anything?" People laugh politely. I'm annoyed that Val's siblings pay her out like this all the time. Don't they realise how successful she is? "Anyway, this is not on the program tonight and is a little surprise for my parents, Drs Hilary and Charles Hartman, who most of you know are celebrating their ruby wedding anniversary today. Well…"

"Get on with it!" someone yells from the crowd.

"Well, as I was saying"—Henry laughs, shaking his head—"today appears to be as good enough as any other day for a wedding, and my gorgeous partner Ken, well, we met ten years ago tonight at Mum and Dad's thirtieth anniversary, so we thought…"

And with that, Ken appears with a celebrant, and Christian and Val walk out together to gasps amongst the crowd. It is a simple ceremony, but it is heartfelt. The ceremony leads to their first dance together. Val has a quick dance with Christian before excusing herself.

I'm still standing with Emily and Boyd, who have their arms around each other, looking on at the festivities.

"You knew, and you didn't tell me?" Emily pokes Val in the shoulder when Val finds her way over to us.

"I was sworn to secrecy, honestly."

"Well, you made a good best woman, and I think Hen made a good choice in asking you," Emily concedes, but her tone tells me it's all said in jest.

"I'm sorry. If I get married, I'll make sure my fiancé gets Boyd to be best man." I hear the jest in Val's voice, but I think Emily misses it.

"Did you hear that, Rhys? Boyd's going to be your best man." Emily squeezes my arm as Boyd pats me on the back. Val shakes her head and rolls her eyes before grabbing my hand and dragging me back to the dance floor.

"I should have had you dance with me on *Serenity* if I knew you could actually dance." I try to joke with Val, but it isn't funny. Twirling Val away from me then drawing her back into my arms feels so right.

"You'll have to organise a work do on her," Val quips with a smile.

"Why's that?" I pull her back into me and hold her.

"Well, because come Monday, we go back to being colleagues."

I want to read into Val's melancholy tone, but I could just have misheard her through the sound of the music. I hold her tight as we traverse the dance floor. If I had my way, I'd never let her go.

As the dance ends, we're told it's time for the main auction. Val and I make our way to the front of the dance floor, just in front of the stage.

We're reminded that all proceeds go to the cardiac department at the hospital. The first few items go for above reserve, including the signed football and a private dinner party hosted by a local French chef, which Giles wins, saying it is for his parents. Val bounces on her toes when the item I know she's been waiting for comes up. A week in a luxury bed-and-breakfast in the Tablelands behind Cassowary Point, all fully catered.

"Ladies and gentlemen, do I hear $1,000?" I raise my hand.

"Hey, I want this one! It looks so relaxing." Val squeezes my arm. "I've got visions of spending a week reading and going for walks and, of course, taking time to see my family on either side."

"Well, I want it, too." I shrug.

"$2,000," Val calls out. "When would you use it?"

"$3,000," I yell back. "I could visit clients and then have some leave. I love it up here, remember?"

"$5,000," Val hollers, her arms crossing against her chest, clearly aware the reserve is a little over $4,000.

"You realise you are bidding against your partner?" Giles comes over and places his hands on Val's shoulders.

"I want it. He can just outbid me." She is clearly waiting for the auctioneer to call the items as going once, twice, or whatever he's about to say.

"Did I hear all proceeds were going to the cardiac program at the hospital?" I enquire.

"That's right, sir." The auctioneer holds his hammer against his palm.

"Excellent. $10,000."

There are gasps around the room. Val looks furious. Giles holds her arms down. "Let him have it. He'll take you anyway, you know."

She's almost in tears, and I want to tell her that her brother's right. I want to spend a week with her up here. Heck, I'd spend a lifetime with her up here if she'd have me.

"Going once, twice, three times, you are out, Miss?" Val nods. "Sold to the dashing young man who looks so like a Hartman, he might as well be one."

The room erupts in laughter and applause.

"Thank you, Rhys." Hillary comes over and draws me in for a hug. "You'll get a tax receipt, don't worry."

"My uncle died from a coronary, so it's a cause close to my heart, pardon the pun," I tell her.

Val still looks upset by the turn of events.

"Well, tell me when you both will be up for your week away. I'm just glad I'll get to see you both again soon. Imagine in winter with a wood fire going... It will be perfect for you two to practice making grandsons."

"Thanks, Mum." Val rolls her eyes.

The auction continues, Charlie bidding for rock climbing lessons, which he looks relieved to lose to someone Giles explains is his registrar from work.

It's a joyous feeling around the space, but Val still seems upset.

"No hard feelings?" I pull her towards the bar to grab us both another drink.

"I was looking forward to a week there reading and walking. I hope you enjoy it," she whispers.

"Come here." I pull her in for a hug, and I almost melt at how perfect it feels.

Our hug is broken by the bartender asking for our drink order.

"Well done, Rhys." Henry comes over and shakes my hand. We all move away from the bar towards an empty table. "Glad I'll be seeing both of you again soon. Ken and I spent a weekend up there before Christmas, and it's the most perfect place."

"Oh yes," Ken adds, holding his new husband's hand. "The bed's super comfortable, and there are lots of flat surfaces, if you get my drift." Henry winks at Ken.

The auction has finished, and the compere announces that it's time for some slow dancing. I want to tell Val that I bought the item for her, but she knocks back her champagne before almost slamming the glass on the table we're standing at.

"Do I get this one, too, or are you still gloating at outbidding me and looking for a sexy doctor to dance with?" Val asks, her eyes wet with unshed tears.

I hate to think I'm the one who's put them there.

"I'd be honoured. I haven't noticed any sexy doctors around tonight." My eyes don't leave hers as I take her hand, and we walk back towards the dance floor.

"Oh, come on, the place is swimming in them."

"I must have been looking somewhere else."

I'm not sure if it is the emotion from the auction or the fact that we're holding each other so close, but before long, we simply look into each other's eyes, and our lips meet. It feels as though every neuron in my body sparks, all of me aware that my lips are joined to Val's.

It's not a chaste kiss, either. Before long, tongues twirl inside each other's mouths, and hands grab onto each other's backsides, trying to draw the other one closer. It feels amazing, and the electricity that cascades through my body is like nothing I have ever experienced.

I couldn't say what song was playing, or who was nearby, or even if we were still moving to the music, but we are creating our own harmony of moans as we devour each other.

"Get a room, you two." Boyd and Emily sidle up to us, breaking the spell.

Suddenly, Val and I are at arm's length from each other with a look of shock on both of our faces.

"Shit. I'm sorry. That was uncalled for. Fuck. Um. Fuck. Sorry." And I escape from her as fast as I can.

# 19

# Val

I'VE NEVER BEEN KISSED LIKE THIS. I EXPECTED RHYS'S LIPS to be tender in their approach to mine, but there's a ferociousness behind them, too. It's as if neither of us can get enough of the other. I couldn't tell you what song the band is playing or how many other people are on the dance floor. It's only Rhys and me that matter.

The give and take of our tongues as we each try to get as close to the other as possible sees my ruby thong drenched. I can feel Rhys' arousal pushing against my stomach as one of his hands clasps the back of my head, the other stroking up and down my bare back.

My hands are wrapped around Rhys' back, holding him as tight as I can. I don't want him to escape. He's my person, and I need to let him know this.

"Get a room, you two." Boyd laughs as he and Emily come to dance beside us. The spell is broken.

Suddenly, Rhys and I are at arm's length from each other with a look of shock on both of our faces.

After some mumbling words of regret, Rhys escapes from me as fast as he can.

"I've got him. You look after your sister." Emily points at me as she turns and races after Rhys.

My hands shake, and large tears tumble from my eyes. Boyd pulls me to his chest, my makeup smearing down his white shirt. All I can do is sob, thinking about what a fool I've been and how everything has turned out opposite to the way I had planned.

"Come on, stinky, deep breaths." Boyd pats my back. "You're probably the last Hartman to kiss on this dance floor, after all."

"Yeah, but—" I sob. "Come Monday, the fantasy ends, and he will forget about me while I try to mend a broken heart..."

Boyd has guided me to the side of the marquee, grabbing a bottle of water from which I take a sip. Before long, Emily is back.

"Hurry, he's packing. Get up there and tell him," she demands, dragging me towards the marquee entrance.

"Tell him what?" I manage between sobs.

"That you love him, idiot." Emily all but shakes my shoulders.

I look at my best friend as she and my brother gesture for me to hurry. I don't think I have ever moved as fast as I do in this moment.

Mum reaches a hand towards me as she breaks away from a conversation she's having just inside the entrance to the marquee.

"Not now, Mother!" I yell as I run past her, slipping off my shoes and throwing them to the side, not caring where they land.

I head inside and see Rosa, Emily's mum, bouncing a wide awake Issy on her hip. She says nothing as I race up the stairs, almost tripping on my gown. I fling my bedroom door open just as Rhys zips his bag.

"Rhys, don't go, please," I pant as I try to catch my breath.

"I have to." He looks at the ceiling. I suspect to stop tears from falling down his face. "I can't do this until Monday. It's not an act, and it's too damn painful. I haven't had to act all weekend."

"Would you stay if I told you that contract was null and void and that the other party had developed feelings, rather, um, powerful feelings..." I blurt, as if I'm standing in front of a judge determined to be heard.

"Val," Rhys sighs. "No more fooling, no more lies. Those kisses..."

"They were real, so very real and so very, very heartfelt, and I never imagined this ever happening, but I've fallen head over heels in love with you."

Rhys drops the handles of his bag and just stares at me. "You have? I mean, you keep talking about the Monday, and I keep thinking that it is an act and... you, wow. You love me?"

"I do." More tears slide down my cheeks as I chuckle. "I mean, I never meant to, but it, like, happened. I haven't had to act at all."

"Can you pinch me, please?" Rhys whispers.

"Why?" I croak.

"So I know this isn't a dream." Rhys swipes his thumbs under my eyes, wiping away my tears. "I dreamt about you all night. To wake up with you this morning, doing what I had dreamt about..."

"You feel it, too?"

"Of course I do." He looks shocked that I can even question his feelings. "I adore you and have since you first stepped foot on *Serenity*. Shit, even before then. The retreat was partly my idea, because I wanted to spend some time with you and get to know you, but I was so tongue-tied around you. That last afternoon, when we talked truths and lies, I wanted my truth to be that I wanted to get to know you more, and then Katherine gathered us together again, and you later asked me to come with you this weekend, and you, you love me?" Rhys is rambling, his eyes wide and a grin forming on his wide open mouth.

"Yes." I nod as we both start laughing.

Our lips meet again. This kiss lacks the finesse from the marquee, but it still displays the passion we feel for each other. I slip Rhys' jacket down his arms, and he lets it fall to the floor before fumbling to undo his cufflinks. I'm working on his shirt buttons as we continue our kisses. Through the window, I can hear the band in full swing and the laughter from the gathered crowd, but my focus is on the man who stands in front of me.

His shirt having joined his jacket on the floor, Rhys focuses on my dress. He manages to untie the straps around my shoulders and gives me a quizzical look as he sees the tape holding my breasts in place.

"Fuck." I almost scream as I rip off the sticky bits. The pain brings fresh tears to my eyes, but Rhys simply moves in and focuses on soothing the skin. He doesn't care that there's adhesive still stuck to the edges of my breasts, focussing on swirling his tongue around my nipples, worshipping the mounds as if they are priceless items he's been searching for and finally found.

Before I know it, he tosses me back on the bed, burying his head under my skirt as he rolls the thong down my legs.

I groan when his tongue glides between my folds, finding my needy clit and circling it. A finger penetrates me, stroking along my front wall and searching for the ridge that he knows will bring me pleasure. Soon, he adds another one and uses a come hither motion whilst sucking on my clit.

"Rhys, I'm..." I can't speak as exhilaration rushes over me, my vaginal walls almost crushing his fingers and my body jerking in release.

He goes to wipe his mouth on his arm, but I cup his cheek and bring his lips to mine, tasting myself on his mouth.

We're both awake this evening, both aware of what is happening, and it is clear we both yearn to show the other how much we mean to each other.

Rhys unfastens his pants and pushes them down his legs along with his briefs. I push him to roll him onto his back before lifting the skirt of my dress and impaling myself on his impressive cock. My eyes close as I sink down and each glorious inch strokes its way inside me.

Neurons fire throughout my body as Rhys grips my hands, our fingers interlocked as we move as one. I hope he sees the same adoration in my eyes that I see in his as I rock back and forth, trying to take him deeper, yearning for another release.

Both of us emit tiny moans and groans, the sounds filling my room with a song I want to sing over and over again. I lean forward and take Rhys' bottom lip between my teeth. He drops one of my hands as he finds my breast again.

Neither of us speaks, but it's as if we can tell the other is close. Too soon, I cry out in ecstasy as a second orgasm rips through me. Rhys isn't far behind me, grunting as he empties himself inside me.

I've had a lot of sex, but never like this. I've never felt this close to someone before. We lie together on my bed, Rhys reaching for a sheet to cover us. Our giggles are interspersed with kisses.

"Your tits are perfect," Rhys whispers. "But it's this curve here..." He traces down my side from my stomach to my hips. "It gets me every time."

"Yeah?" I smile, my bottom lip between my teeth. "I love your shoulders. I could have spent all day on *Serenity* rubbing sunscreen into them."

We carry on with our tales of wonder at each other before there's a knock at the door.

"You two left the party early." Mum stands there with a glass of champagne in her hand.

"Sorry, Mum. We, well, we worked some things out, that's all." I snuggle against Rhys as he strokes my back.

"Hmm. So, Giles and I each owe each other money or something?" Mum smirks.

"Something like that." I place a kiss on Rhys' cheek. "But you were right, he is a keeper."

There's no shame in my family for public displays of affection, and it shouldn't surprise me that my mother is talking to us as we lie mostly naked under a sheet in bed.

Mum goes to close the door before opening it again. "Oh, and Rhys,"

"Yes, Hills?" Rhys looks at me though, instead of my mother, a huge smile on his face.

"You are needed downstairs again. Apparently, you've bought a glass sculpture for $5,000."

"Did you outbid me on that, too?" I ask, rising onto an elbow.

"Guilty, your honour." Rhys laughs. "But it was for you."

"Really?" I melt at his admission.

"Yes. Just like I hoped that we might spend a week together on the Tablelands this winter."

I must have been blind to miss the way both of us were falling for each other, and, perhaps some better communication would not have gone astray, but I was thrilled to be here now with Rhys, and I looked forward to a future together, wherever that may be.

"I love you, Rhys no middle name Evans."

"And I love you, Valerie Hillary Charlotte Hartman."

# Epilogue - Val

*10 years later*

"Come on, Theo. We need to get moving. Can you just step onto the wharf for me, please?" I pinch my lips together as I inwardly smile at Rhys' pleas with our four-year-old who never wants to leave the water. "Come on, mate, there's more chocolate cake at home, and Magma and TomCat are coming tomorrow to stay for a while, and Auntie Myf and Uncle Rob will be here later this week with your other cousins."

"You mean Alice and Nick?"

"That's right, Felix." Rhys ruffles the hair of master seven going on seventeen.

"Magma and TomCat." Theo is up on the deck in no time. I still smile at the names Archie and Alice came up with all those years ago for the grandparents who refused to be called grandma and grandpa.

"When can we go out on *Serenity II* again, Dad?" Nine-year-old Archie is the spitting image of his father, not only in looks but in his introversion. Like his brothers, he loves a day on the ocean.

"Probably not until after the baby comes, Arch," I tell him as he climbs up behind Theo and grabs his hand like the overprotective big brother he is.

"What about next weekend?" Felix waits for me to disembark, always needing to be close by.

"That's Valentine's weekend, Felix." I wrap my spare arm around his scrawny shoulders, placing a kiss on his head.

"And Gammy and Grumpy's party in the big tent?" Theo bounces up and down on the deck as he waits for us.

I smile every time Theo calls my father Grumpy, as he is one of the most laid back men you will ever find. Our family has a history of evolving names over time, and it would seem poor Dad has had a name evolution, too. With so many grandchildren now, I'm not too surprised.

"That's right, Theo." I turn to Rhys. "Darling, can you take Oscar from me?"

"Sure thing, my love." Rhys takes our two-year-old and blows a raspberry on his belly, exposed from his shirt riding up. I need to get the next size up out again; they grow so fast.

"Is that the Valentine's party that I came from?" Archie has heard this story over and over and still loves it.

"That's right, Archie," Rhys smiles at our eldest before turning and whispering in my ear, "The one where Mummy forgot the doctor had removed her IUD without putting in a new one, which is, in my opinion, the best thing your mother has ever forgotten."

"The appointment had disappeared from my diary, and I had forgotten I needed to go back again. Not that I'm complaining." I plant a kiss on his lips as he helps me climb onto the deck.

"That's why sensible people keep paper diaries." He swats my backside and gives me a wink when I turn to scowl at him.

"You love my nonsensical whims." I place a chaste kiss on his lips. Surrounded by our children, the feeling of love is palpable.

Finally, we're all off *Serenity II* and walking down the pier towards our car.

"Is this baby going to be another boy?" Felix holds my hand. Whereas Archie wouldn't be seen dead holding onto either his father or me, Felix really is my shadow.

"We don't know, Felix. Mummy and Daddy decided not to find out," Rhys tells him, wrestling Oscar onto his shoulders, thus preventing him from getting down and running off. He's the most energetic out of all our sons, and that's saying something.

"I will admit, I would prefer a girl like Issy and Alice and Jess and Layla." Archie sounds like an old soul. Maggie tells me he is just like Rhys was at the same age.

"It might be another boy, Archie. We'll just have to wait and see." Archie reluctantly lets his father drape his arm over his shoulders as we walk along the pier.

"Is it just one baby still?" Theo has wedged himself between Rhys and me and keeps urging us to swing him in the air.

"Oh, Theo, Mummy, and Daddy aren't as smart as Uncle Henry and Uncle Ken or Auntie Emily and Uncle Boyd." I laugh.

We get to the car and start wrangling our sons into their seats.

"Baby in tummy, Mummy," says Oscar as he pats my belly.

"That's right, Oscar." You're going to be a big brother like Archie, Felix, and Theo.

"So, when is it coming again?" Felix asks as he clicks in his seatbelt.

"Well, Mummy is due in two weeks on her birthday, and you boys all came at least a week late, so it could even be a March baby like you, Felix." Rhys checks Theo is buckled in safely.

"I'm going to tell Grammy that I'm going to be a fireman." Theo pretends to hold a large hose and spray Archie, who simply rolls his eyes. He's also a Hartman at heart.

"No, Theo, we all have to be lawyers, remember?" Archie admonishes his younger brother.

"No, Archie, just not doctors." Felix is always arguing, and it wouldn't surprise me if he chooses a life in the law like his parents.

"But I want to be a fireman..." Theo's bottom lip starts to wobble, and I know the tears aren't far away.

"You can be a fireman, Theo." I can't help but smile at my four sons as I feel the baby kicking inside of me. Rhys shakes his head as we head out of the car park towards home.

It's been a gorgeous day on the water. Rhys and Archie caught a fish whilst Oscar and Theo napped and Felix and I read a book.

*Serenity* would never be large enough for all of us once Felix was born, but we did some beautiful dancing both above and below deck on her and still head out on her replacement most weekends. It's a life I could almost never have dreamt of.

Navigating a new relationship with a colleague was challenging enough, but telling him three weeks after our trip to Cassowary Point for my parents' ruby wedding anniversary that I was pregnant was unexpected for both of us.

Rhys didn't balk at the idea. Instead, he swung me around the deck of my small cottage in Brisbane until I vomited all over him, and then he helped me clean myself up before even worrying about himself.

Each pregnancy has been somewhat of a surprise. They probably shouldn't have been, seeing we both have high sex drives and have only relied on breastfeeding as contraception for ten years. As for marriage, Rhys has finally worn me down. I tried to argue that if we weren't married, we couldn't get divorced. And yes, I am very well aware of the poor logic of my reasoning, seeing we've been in a domestic partnership for almost ten years now.

I think I knew it before the gala I brought Rhys to as my fake boyfriend, but our feelings for each other have never been a work of fiction.

"Mm..." I moan as Rhys spoons me, his fingers still playing with my sensitive nipples. "That was amazing. You sure know how to show me you love me."

"I thought it was my shoulder rubs you loved?" Rhys nips gently at my shoulders, causing a shiver to creep down my back. Even in our post orgasmic bliss, I feel like I could do it all again.

"I love it when you rub all of me, especially my insides, with your phenomenal cock."

"Insatiable woman!" I turn my head, and Rhys and I share little kisses. I'm thrilled we still find time for intimacy after all these years, even if it is after midnight and we have a gala ball this evening.

"I've never heard you complain." I turn and ignore the sharp pain in my abdomen. This baby loves to press hands and feet everywhere, and for the last week, I've been in some form of discomfort. "Do you mind this baby will be the only one born in wedlock?"

"Considering I've been asking for almost ten years now, and we hyphenated our names when Archie was born?" Rhys laughs as he strokes my cheek "Seriously though, if you're getting cold feet, we can still delay it. I mean, it's only a piece of paper, and by law, we are well and truly married de facto."

"No, it will be perfect." I smile, taking in a large breath. "Mum and Dad's golden anniversary, Hen and Ken's tenth. Em's mum has sewn the most amazing dress, and even though I look like I've got a watermelon in my stomach, I'll get to tell everyone again how much I adore you."

"I adore you too, my sexy love. The ruby-red number is still my favourite." Rhys rubs his nose against mine. My belly feels like it's in the way, but he doesn't mind.

"I was five months pregnant with Theo at the last gala, but I did like that blue dress that matched your eyes." The light that shines through the gap at the side of the curtain is enough for me to almost see the depth of my almost husband's eyes.

"You looked stunning," Rhys whispers. "But then again, you always do."

"You are such a keeper. Thanks for helping with the marquee today."

"We had lots of help, remember?" He laughs as he rolls onto his back and I weave my legs through his. He's better than any body pillow I've tried. "Theo is just enthralled with the big tent and was sad I wouldn't let him camp in there tonight."

"It was a family effort, wasn't it? Millie and Mia were a great help, and Adam's a lovely guy. Bridget seems to think so, too, but I know Giles is pretending it isn't happening. Seeing Mum fuss around the hanging of the lights was funny. I think we've worked out how to do it after all these years."

"Your parents only sold us this house because they knew we'd keep the Valentine's gala going." Rhys turns his head to me, a huge smile still on his face.

"Probably. That, and they knew we'd fill it with kids. Do you still want five, or could you go a sixth?" I stroke my finger up and down his chest.

"Well, Ms 'I've left it too late for five', we can talk about this in a few months. I mean, with your family's propensity for multiple births..." Rhys laughs as our fingers intertwine. "You know I won't mind if we have five sons or even six or seven. Although, Boyd keeps recommending the guy who did his vasectomy. I'll admit, making them has been so much fun. Now, come on, we better get some sleep."

"Mm... Although Ken, Hen, Boyd, and Em had some help with theirs, I suppose. I still can't believe Em and Boyd implanted a single embryo, and after all those years, they managed it on their own as well." I snuggled into Rhys' shoulder.

"We've been so blessed, all of us really. Now, sleep." He turns and gives me a gentle kiss on my lips.

"It's so good seeing Myf and Rob again. I still wish they'd move up here, too." I've yawned all day and had to sit and supervise a lot of the marquee decoration because my feet are so swollen, but I'm not at all tired now.

"They're still contemplating it. I know Myf always wanted a sister, and I'm so glad the two of you get along so well." Rhys wriggles, attempting to get comfortable. "Maybe after Rob's next book tour."

"Oh, and darl, Katherine, and Max messaged me to say they arrived safely, as did Janet, Penny, and the kids."

"You need to stop thinking about all these guests. It's after midnight, my love. Come on, sleep."

"Darling..." I rise on my elbow, my voice higher than usual.

"Yes, my love?" Rhys sounds so gentle, even though I know he's tired.

"Can you feel the wetness?"

"You can't possibly be horny again so quickly." Rhys laughs as he rubs my shoulder. "Now, sleep."

"No, I'm serious. I think my waters broke. I might have just gotten myself out of mani-pedi morning with Emily."

"Ladies and Gentlemen. For those who don't know me, I'm Rhys Hartman-Evans, father of four of the terrors running around tonight." I know Rhys is nervous, but he's a lot less shy after living with me for ten years.

"I'm not a terror." Archie stands with his hands on his hips.

"Sorry, Archie, you're the exception proving the rule." Rhys shakes his head. "Don't worry, all the kids will be back in the house soon. We just need them here for this bit. Um, this isn't on your program, and we haven't told anyone, except for, well, my best friend, Boyd, and his gorgeous wife, Emily. If it's not our four sons causing havoc, it's Emily and Boyd's seven-year-old triplets, and, hey, if you can tell Hughie and Dewie, I mean Hugh and Eddie apart, please let me know."

The way Rhys stands with his hand on my shoulder draws a silent sigh of contentment from my lips.

"Also joining us are my dazzling sister, Myf, and my other best mate, Rob. Their two kids are very well behaved, and I think I need tips from them, which they could give if they moved up here as we've begged. Now, Valerie, the beautiful, gorgeous, exquisite mother of our children, my precious darling, my love, my everything, is the youngest, and I must say, sexiest of all the Hartman children."

It was lovely glancing out and seeing Giles and Bridget and Henry and Ken in each other's arms, no doubt Bridget and Ken thinking they had married the sexiest of the Hartman children. Boyd still made it abundantly clear how much he adored Emily after all these years.

"First, happy golden anniversary, Charlie and Hills, the best out-laws a man could ask for. And happy tenth anniversary to Hen and Ken. You both ruined things by not calling Jess and Liam 'Jen' and 'Len', but never mind. To the magnificent Millie and her fiancé Adam—welcome to the family and good to see the ambos, I mean paramedics represented, too, Adam. Seriously though, mate, glad you've found the women of the law are hotter."

"Speak for yourself!" I hear Giles yell out. "I still haven't forgiven my sister for convincing my beautiful daughter to study law. It's not too late to change either, petal. But hey, Theo's told me tonight he's going to be a doctor like his favourite uncles, so that's something at least."

And here was me thinking he was going to be a fireman. I smile, thinking back on the last ten years, and at the same time wishing my husband-to-be would hurry up.

"Sorry, I'm a little tired. You see, last night as I was trying to convince my gorgeous wife-to-be to go to sleep, the most beautiful baby girl you could ever imagine decided she was going to arrive a week ahead of schedule, at least giving two of her grandparents the elusive Valentine's Day baby they always chased. I suspect beautiful Freya here just wanted to be in on tonight's party. Thanks, Maggie and Tom, for being here. I'm glad you had to put up with Oscar rolling around in your bed last night. Anyhoo, and that is prime legal speak for all you doctors out there, ten years ago on this very special night..."

And that is how I married the one true love of my life, Rhys Hartman-Evans, co-creator of our five beautiful children. Rhys is the most wonderful father, lover, and husband and still has several clients he helps with their maritime issues. I now split my time between a few family law cases and working at the local Women's Legal Centre, which I love, as well as chasing after the five children I never dreamt I'd be blessed with. The university keeps begging me to lecture and, who knows, I might get around to writing this PhD thesis on the relationships of practitioners of family law and become a doctor after all.

I never found out if Mum or Giles coughed up after their bet ten years ago, but I suspect the whole family agrees that, in the end, Rhys and I are the winners, anyway.

Bonus scenes for all books are available at jezabelnightingale.com

# A Note from Jez

Way back before a global pandemic was even something that most of us would have considered, I got the bug for writing and sharing my work with others.

My first short stories were published online. I read through them now with a slight cringe factor—they had some great ideas, but language wise, they could have been executed differently!

The site I was publishing on has several themed competitions each year. My first 'big break' was with Fiction v Reality, which is where the Hartman characters came from. This 18,000 word short story won the Valentine's Competition in 2021. It was unexpected and spurred me to keep writing.

This version is quite different to the short story that precedes it. Scenes have been deleted, many added, and Rhys gets his say in his voice!

Several people have asked if this is the end of the Hartmans. It is for the moment, but there are some stories that keep telling me they want to be told, who knows some of the Hartman-adjacent characters might get their tales one of these days!

Thanks for all the love and encouragement you've shown with this series. I hope you'll enjoy what's coming next!

## I hear you like cake...

So do I! Several of the cake recipes mentioned in this book are available on this Pinterest board:

# Acknowledgments

Thank you to everyone who has read and reviewed this book. Have you reviewed it yet? Please do. Ratings and reviews help get the word out and let other readers discover new works from emerging authors like myself.

To my ARC readers- you are amazing. I love the gentle feedback you supply, especially when it makes me think and change things for the future.

My editorial team of Sarah and Cheyenne. These ladies have unique insight into the workings of my brain, and yes, it can be chaotic at times! Both make me a better writer and for this I am truly grateful.

Kristin always brings the cover goods and is amazing at coming up with what I am thinking about but can't put into words. I can come to her with several possible cover photos and her advice as to what will work better is a huge help.

To Dr Nightingale for being the biggest leader of my cheer squad. You listen to storyline ideas and never question my sanity. Thanks for always making sure my water bottle is full! And to my big babies, you still don't know Mummy writes this stuff... maybe one day!

# Also by Jezabel Nightingale

### The Hartman Family Series
The Heart Switch

A Meeting of Minds

Kidding Around

Fiction v Reality

### The Bayview Monarchs
Tackling Love Once More

### Lovemore Gap
Finding Love

*Coming February 2025*

### Standalone Titles
Secret Santa

# About the Author

Jezabel Nightingale is an emerging author of contemporary romance. She wears so many hats, including nurse, mother, wife, writer, and scholar. In her spare time, you'll find her cheering on AFL football, in the kitchen baking a cake, or reading a spicy romance novel. It is not unusual to find a gin and tonic in her hand, or something chocolatey in her vicinity. She will blame these vices for her overuse of exclamation marks and commas, because, why not?

She lives on the East Coast of Australia with Dr Nightingale, her spunkrat of a husband, her cats, and her kids who keep popping home, despite officially having moved out.

After publishing short stories online for several years, this is her fourth novel.

Manufactured by Amazon.ca
Acheson, AB

15879106R00129